MAY, 1982   TO BE RETURNED
TO GLENN ROTHBART

WELFARE EFFECTS
OF TRADE RESTRICTIONS

A Case Study of the
U.S. Footwear Industry

ECONOMIC THEORY AND MATHEMATICAL ECONOMICS

Consulting Editor: Karl Shell

UNIVERSITY OF PENNSYLVANIA
PHILADELPHIA, PENNSYLVANIA

Franklin M. Fisher and Karl Shell. The Economic Theory of Price Indices: *Two Essays on the Effects of Taste, Quality, and Technological Change*

Luis Eugenio Di Marco (Ed.). International Economics and Development: *Essays in Honor of Raúl Presbisch*

Erwin Klein. Mathematical Methods in Theoretical Economics: *Topological and Vector Space Foundations of Equilibrium Analysis*

Paul Zarembka (Ed.). Frontiers in Econometrics

George Horwich and Paul A. Samuelson (Eds.). Trade, Stability, and Macroeconomics: *Essays in Honor of Lloyd A. Metzler*

W. T. Ziemba and R. G. Vickson (Eds.). Stochastic Optimization Models in Finance

Steven A. Y. Lin (Ed.). Theory and Measurement of Economic Externalities

David Cass and Karl Shell (Eds.). The Hamiltonian Approach to Dynamic Economics

R. Shone. Microeconomics: *A Modern Treatment*

C. W. J. Granger and Paul Newbold. Forecasting Economic Time Series

Michael Szenberg, John W. Lombardi, and Eric Y. Lee. Welfare Effects of Trade Restrictions: *A Case Study of the U.S. Footwear Industry*

In preparation

Haim Levy and Marshall Sarnat (Eds.). Financial Decision Making under Uncertainty

Yasuo Murata. Mathematics for Stability and Optimization of Economic Systems

Alan S. Blinder and Philip Friedman (Eds.). Natural Resources, Uncertainty, and General Equilibrium Systems: *Essays in Memory of Rafael Lusky*

WELFARE EFFECTS
OF TRADE RESTRICTIONS

A Case Study of the U.S. Footwear Industry

MICHAEL SZENBERG
JOHN W. LOMBARDI

Department of Economics, Finance, and Public Policy
Long Island University
Brooklyn, New York

ERIC Y. LEE

Department of Economics
Fairleigh Dickinson University
Madison, New Jersey

ACADEMIC PRESS   New York   San Francisco   London   1977
A Subsidiary of Harcourt Brace Jovanovich, Publishers

ACADEMIC PRESS, INC.
111 Fifth Avenue, New York, New York 10003

United Kingdom Edition published by
ACADEMIC PRESS, INC. (LONDON) LTD.
24/28 Oval Road, London NW1

Library of Congress Cataloging in Publication Data

Szenberg, Michael.
    Welfare effects of trade restrictions.

    (Economic theory and mathematical economics series)
    Bibliography: p.
    1.   Boots and shoes—Trade and manufacture—United
States.   2.   Restraint of trade—United States—Case
studies.   3.   Tariff on boots and shoes—United States.
I.   Lombardi, John W., joint author.   II.   Lee, Eric
Youngkoo, joint author.   III.   Title.
HD9787.U45S93   338.4'7'6853100973   77-7486
ISBN 0—12—681050—8

To our delightful children
Naomi, Avi
Mary, Allison
Ruth, Lydia, and Michael

CONTENTS

FOREWORD

There could hardly be a more propitious time to publish this book on the United States footwear industry. This sector, which has been the focal point of protectionist pressures in the country since the late 1960s, has recently been the subject of policy attention by the International Trade Commission and by the President. Early this year the Commission found by a unanimous 6–0 vote that the shoe industry was being seriously injured by imports and recommended a sliding tariff rate that would increase—as imports increased—from the present level of about 10% to 40%. However, the President did not accept this recommendation but instead directed his trade negotiators to seek a voluntary export constraint program on the part of Taiwan and South Korea. If these negotiations follow the typical pattern, they will be lengthy but eventually lead to some form of quantitative restrictions of imports of footwear from these countries. Should the Congress not agree with the President's action in the case, it can override it by a majority vote of both the House and Senate and put into effect the recommendation of the Commission. This provision has the effect of ensuring some type of restrictive action in a politically powerful industry such as shoes.

The footwear industry vividly illustrates the hard economic and social decisions the United States must make as the world becomes increasingly interdependent through trade. Increasing exports in fairly low-skill, labor-intensive manufacturing lines is an important manner by which income levels in developing countries can be raised and the degree of income inequality between rich and poor nations reduced. Exports have in the past been a key engine of growth for the presently developed countries. Not only do workers abroad benefit from greater imports of shoes into the United States, but American consumers gain by lower shoe prices and a greater variety of shoe styles from which to choose. On the other hand, rapid rises in imports can cause significant losses of jobs and idling of capital capacity in this country.

Economists in the past were inclined to dismiss these losses by pointing out that they would disappear in the long-run. This is not only a socially cavalier attitude but bad economics. Society continually compares present and future costs and benefits through the interest-rate mechanism. While one can cogently argue that the market rate of interest is not the proper rate to use, there is no doubt that discounting is the proper way to compare present costs and future benefits. The authors do follow this procedure and their estimates include the social costs due to the unemployment caused by greater shoe imports.

Although there is no necessary reason why benefits should outweigh costs in any particular industry when imports increase as foreign costs fall relative to United States' costs or United States' duties are decreased, the very significant conclusion reached by the authors is that consumer benefits outweigh workers' losses in the shoe industry at any plausible discount rate. This result is reached on the basis of a very careful, economically sound investigation of the shoe industry and cannot be lightly dismissed. It is, of course, hard for the affected workers to accept this conclusion as the basis of the social policy that should be followed since they are not in fact fully compensated for their own losses. Through no fault of their own they are being asked to bear the burden of import adjustment costs.

Most proponents of a liberal United States trade policy would accept the desirability of minimizing or even eliminating the economic costs imposed on workers from greater imports. This could be accomplished by complete compensation or the use of import controls enabling present workers to maintain their jobs until their retirement or a decision to quit voluntarily. What liberal traders object to is the fact that the solutions proposed by protectionists seek not only to achieve this result but to ensure jobs in the industry for future entrants into the labor force. In a real sense these solutions condemn these future workers to a life of low wages and persistent unemployment. The situation is similar to some of our environmental issues. If we use up our present resources too rapidly, the income levels of future generations may fall. Similarly, if we fail to adjust to world economic conditions, future generations may find their income levels needlessly low. Income levels of American workers will continue to grow at a satisfactory pace only if these workers are shifted from low wage, low productivity-growth industries to skill-intensive, high technology sectors.

What seems required is a program that leads to *adjustment* and not the indefinite maintenance of the status quo. While not an easy problem to solve, it is by no means impossible. A system of incentives or penalties is required to make sure that, as present workers voluntarily leave the labor force, firms unable to meet international competition close down. Some limits of the speed by which imports can increase in economically weak industries may also be justified. In this respect, automatic devices such as tariff quotas seem more justified than voluntary or mandatory quantitative controls. The latter devices are likely either to prove ineffective or be captured by protectionists to maintain existing conditions.

ROBERT E. BALDWIN
UNIVERSITY OF WISCONSIN, MADISON

PREFACE

From about 1955 to 1975, imports of nonrubber footwear into the United States increased markedly; they rose from an annual average of a mere 10 million pairs in the mid-1950s to over 300 million pairs in 1975. In terms of the share of the market for nonrubber footwear, imports supplied only 2% of United States consumption in the mid-1950s and account for about 33% of the total consumption in the 1970s. Japan, Italy, Taiwan, Spain, and, more recently, Brazil, have been the major suppliers.

Nonrubber footwear is currently dutiable on entry into the United States under 23 Tariff Schedule of the United States (TSUS) items, but the bulk of the imports are dutiable under four major categories. The United States import duty applicable to certain leather footwear for men and boys (TSUS 700.35) is 8.5% *ad valorem,* while the rates on certain leather footwear for women and misses (TSUS 700.43 and 700.45) are 15 and 10%, respectively. The rate on footwear with uppers of plastic, largely supported vinyl uppers for women and misses (TSUS 700.55), is 6%. The United States nonrubber footwear industry, labor, and other protectionist groups have been clamoring for much higher tariff protection than is now provided under the Trade Expansion Act of 1962.

Indeed, the current plight of the industry was dramatically highlighted in early 1977 by President Jimmy Carter's rejection of drastic restrictions on shoe imports proposed by the International Trade Commission. He decided instead to try to negotiate agreements with exporting countries to limit their shipments to the United States market. He said that he was ''very reluctant'' to restrict international trade in any way. ''For 40 years the U.S. has worked for the reduction of trade barriers around the world, and we are continuing to pursue this goal because it is the surest long-range way to create jobs here and abroad'' (*Wall Street Journal,* April 4, 1977). By this, the President sustained Gerald Ford's decision in 1976 rejecting protectionist measures of further increases in the tariff rate or imposition of import quotas. Perhaps this decision represents a major step in the direction of reversing increasing United States protectionist tendencies that became apparent in March 1976 following the adoption of trade restrictive measures in the form of import quotas on specialty steel.

The principal objective of this study is to analyze and evaluate the welfare effects of removing trade restrictions on United States imports of nonrubber footwear through the product and employment markets. It estimates the net gains to footwear consumers and the resultant earning losses of workers displaced by the trade liberalization. Special attention is given to the structural characteristics of the industry and its adjustment experience to import competition.

The general organization of this book is as follows: Chapters I and II examine in detail the structural characteristics of the domestic footwear industry and its degree of competition. In Chapter III, the analytical framework for estimating the welfare effects of removing trade restrictions on imported footwear is developed using a consumer surplus approach. The relevant parameters needed in evaluating the foregoing effects of import restrictions on the domestic industry are then estimated empirically. Chapter IV evaluates the trade adjustment assistance experience of the footwear industry.

While the metholology of this study is primarily empirical, its orientation is conditioned by the accessibility and nature of data relevant to the industry. This is a problem that plagues all micro studies. We need not, for example, always treat the products of the nonrubber footwear industry and the imports as a single homogeneous group, since in reality there are several categories of nonrubber footwear, such as men's dress/casual shoes, women's dress/casual shoes, work shoes, athletic shoes, and slippers. These in effect constitute separate markets involving distinct policy decisions. The obvious criterion for realistically dividing the industry into groups is made on the basis of negligible cross-elasticities such as men's versus women's and adults' versus children's, which would indicate that the relevant commodities are distinctly separate and justifiably treated as such. However, even this refinement is not completely free of difficulties. It does not, for example, allow us to analyze to any great extent the influence of fashion and product differentiation on the demand for footwear. Another major difficulty in proceeding to more meaningful levels of disaggregation lies in the nature of the data. That is, data do not seem to be specific, varied, or timely enough to permit detailed examination of the major thrusts of import competition and their impact on the domestic industry. Production and imports of different types of shoes are tabulated for rather broad groups—too broad in relation to the many different types, constructions, and qualities of shoes available in the market to permit all desirable analyses. A major handicap, for example, is the lack of data on domestic production of vinyl shoes—a serious shortcoming since approximately half of all imported shoes are vinyl.

The generation of suitable time series poses difficulties in compiling statistical data that are consistent over time in terms of definition, classification, comparability, etc. Vinyl import data have been available only since 1964; prior to 1960, imports of women's and misses' nonrubber footwear were often lumped together with children's and infants' imports; some categories of footwear are not specified by sex of wearer; athletic and work shoes are combined for earlier years but are separated in later years; and tariff schedules display substantial variations over time.

There are four major findings of this study.

1. The total United States demand for footwear, including imports, seems to be quite insensitive to price changes. At the same time, the demand for imported footwear is much more elastic, as indicated by an import price elasticity of -1.5. There appears to be a high degree of substitutability between imported and domestic footwear, as shown by the high cross-elasticities obtained. The import demand for men/boys footwear is found to be much less price elastic than that for the women/misses group.

2. The supply of domestically produced footwear is highly price elastic; this indicates the rapid adjustment of the industry to changes in demand. The footwear industry at the manufacturing stage approximates the classical concept of competition. The usual characteristics of many largely atomistic firms, easy entry and exit, owner management, constant technology, negligible economies of scale, and the almost complete absence of price leadership and/or price fixing are all conspicuously present.

3. Cost/benefit analysis reveals that elimination of the current 10% tariff rate on imported footwear will confer total consumer welfare gains of approximately $162.2 million based on an 8% discount rate, while producing social costs of about $83.51 million in the form of lost earnings by displaced workers. This leaves net social welfare gains of approximately $78.69 mil-

lion, which clearly indicates that the gain to society as a whole associated with trade liberalization will more than compensate for any loss incurred by affected groups. That is, the gainers can easily compensate the losers, implying that adjustment to the injured workers and firms out of the general tax revenue would be justified on economic‚grounds.

4.   It is recognized that while the removal of trade restrictions leads to generally desirable outcomes, this may be painful to accomplish in practice. The many unpleasant problems of adjustment fall heavily on a relatively small segment of society—those engaged in protected production—while the gains are reaped by all members of society. Movement to freer trade, however, need not be prevented on the basis of this argument. A number of compensatory schemes, of which trade adjustment assistance is the most recent innovation, can be implemented to offset in part the problems of transition.

ACKNOWLEDGMENTS

The research upon which this book is based was supported by the Bureau of International Labor Affairs (BILA) of the United States Department of Labor. This support is most warmly appreciated. It goes without saying that the responsibility for the points of view expressed here are entirely our own.

We received immeasurable assistance from a number of people. We are grateful to Dr. William Dewald, the former Director of Research of BILA, currently Professor of Economics at Ohio State University, who encouraged and helped us to initiate this project. His successor, Dr. Harry Grubert and his staff, Steb Hipple, Larry Wipf, and Donald Rousslang, provided a highly constructive and detailed review of the study. Their efforts and suggestions are greatly appreciated. Professors Bernard Newton, Chairman of the Department of Economics at Long Island University and Elizabeth Bogan of Fairleigh Dickinson University read through the manuscript and made helpful comments. A special recognition is due to Professors Sheldon Novack, Chairman of the Business Economics, Finance, and Public Policy Department, Philip Wolitzer, Chairman of the Accounting Department, and Albert E. Johnson, Dean of the School of Business Administration at Long Island University for their cooperation at various phases of our work.

We have benefited from consultations with many officials of various companies and agencies of the footwear industry, particularly Stanley Neufeld,

Harvey Bush, and Sundar Shetty, Manager of the Bureau of Statistical Services, American Footwear Industries Association.

A special note of thanks goes to Professor Victor R. Fuchs, Codirector of the National Bureau of Economic Research for his many kindnesses, advice, and counsel.

Our thanks also go to those who cheerfully assisted us. Among them are Suellen Manning, Yehoshua Livnat, Arnon Ben-Ami, Salah Danial, and Charles Wainhouse.

Finally, we must thank our wives Miriam, Mary, and Maria, and our children without whom there would be no book at all.

I

STRUCTURE OF THE UNITED STATES FOOTWEAR INDUSTRY

Economic theory and industrial experience suggest the importance, among others, of the following elements determining firm behavior and industry performance: the degree of seller concentration and the size distribution of footwear producers, vertical production arrangements, economies of scale in production, and patterns of entry and exit. These four structural dimensions are investigated because they may help shed light on the workability of competition in this market. This chapter examines the footwear industry's pattern of development, the role of imports, and the first two structural elements. Chapter II will treat the latter two characteristics of the industry.

1. THE PATTERN OF DEVELOPMENT, 1954–1974

A better understanding of many of the forces that have helped to mold the footwear industry and of its present-day organization is achieved by reviewing its development pattern from the early 1950s,

1

when footwear imports were negligible, to 1974, when these reached prominence in the economy.

TABLE I-1

Development of the United States Nonrubber Footwear
Industry in Selected Years

Year	Domestic production (million pairs)	Value of shipments (million dollars)	Value added by manufactures (million dollars)	Employment
1947	483.1	1788	782	229,303
1954	473.4	1845	941	219,375
1958	524.3	2092	1086	215,311
1963	604.3	2249	1215	201,728
1967	599.9	2771	1526	198,500
1972	548.3	3161	1710	167,800
1973	488.2	3047	a	a

[a]Not available.
SOURCE: United States Bureau of the Census, *Census of Manufactures* (various years), *Current Industrial Reports* (annual issues).

Table I-1 summarizes the principal dimensions of the domestic industry's development. The decline in production of the domestic industry (in terms of number of pairs produced) has not been distributed evenly over all the major footwear categories. Moreover, the declining trend of several major footwear groups is not without its reverse movements. The decline has predominantly affected the largest components of footwear output—women's shoes and, to a smaller extent, misses' shoes, and children's and infants' shoes. Production of men's dress shoes and of youths' and boys' shoes has remained relatively stable over time. On the other hand, athletic footwear and work shoes have experienced gains in production as indicated in Figure I-1.

The value of footwear shipments increased from $1.8 billion in 1954 to $3.0 billion, an 160-fold gain. Value added rose from $941 million to $1.7 billion, an 180-fold jump. A different picture emerges, however, when physical output and employment figures are examined. Physical output of footwear (in pairs) recorded gains until 1963, and thereafter fell from 604 to 488 million pairs in 1973, while employment declined steadily since 1954 from 219,400 to 167,800.

Turning now to an examination of the footwear industry's posi-

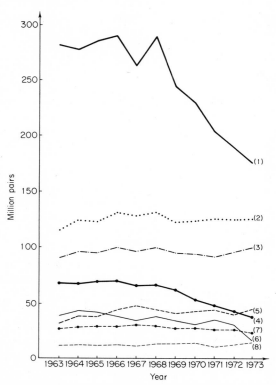

Figure I-1. United States production of nonrubber footwear by major types (pairs). LEGEND: (1) women's shoes; (2) men's shoes; (3) men's dress shoes; (4) children's and infants' shoes; (5) work shoes; (6) misses' shoes; (7) youths' and boys' shoes; (8) athletic shoes.

tion in the economic order, we find that in 1972 the industry accounted for about 0.4% of value added and 0.9% of employment of the total manufacturing activity in the United States. This represents a sizable loss over all three of these categories about two decades earlier. On the other hand, value added as a percent of gross national product (GNP) has remained stable since 1954, as indicated in Table I-2.

From the standpoint of capital outlay, the performance of the footwear industry falls far short in comparison with most other manufacturing industries. In 1972 the ratio of capital expenditure to value added was only about 2.1%,[1] while for all manufacturing the ratio was

[1]In 1972 capital expenditures stood at $35 million. Note that several leading

TABLE I-2

Development of the Nonrubber Footwear Industry as a Percentage
of All Manufacturing and Gross National
Product (GNP) in Selected Years

Year	Percent of value of shipments	Percent of value added by manufactures	Value added (percent of GNP)	Percent of industrial employment
1947	a	1.1	0.4	1.6
1954	a	0.8	0.2	1.4
1958	a	0.8	0.2	1.4
1963	0.5	0.6	0.2	1.2
1967	0.5	0.6	0.2	1.1
1972	0.4	0.5	0.2	0.9

aNot available.

SOURCE: United States Bureau of the Census, *Census of Manufactures* (various years), *Current Industrial Reports* (annual issues).

about 8%. No wonder, then, that industrywide efforts to counteract imports through basic technological change have been very slow.[2] A government survey of productivity gains during 1957 and 1970 for twenty-seven industries reports the shoe industry as last, with only a slight gain in productivity (*Business Week,* June 10, 1972, p. 68). In the period 1960–1971, the industry experienced an average annual rate of change in the output per man-hour[3] index of only 0.3% [68, p. 51].

2.   THE ROLE OF IMPORTS

This section will consider several aspects of the increasing import trend of nonrubber footwear into the United States, namely the geographic and type distribution.

multiplant firms are currently undergoing a strong technological push to automate production processes. This may confer comparative advantages in categories of footwear that has been imported until now.

[2]For a descriptive analysis of the problems and prospects of high-productivity systems in the footwear industry, see Jacks [26]. A more analytical investigation is found in Cohn [18]. Currently, Duchesneau and Mandell [21] are investigating the adoption of production technology in certain large-scale companies in the footwear industry. See also Priebe [37].

[3]The United States footwear industry still has the highest man-hour productivity among the major footwear producers. However, this advantage is more than offset by the hourly labor cost disadvantage, which is enough to give the United States the highest unit labor cost, except for West Germany. See Cohn [18, p. 9].

The footwear share of the total value of United States imports for consumption constituted only about 1.4% in 1973. In terms of domestic footwear consumption, the import share shows a dramatic unbroken rise to about 40% (in pairage terms) and 24% (in value terms) in the same year.

Table I-3 and Appendix Tables I-A–I-E describe the expansion of American footwear imports in terms of their geographical distribution over the period 1963–1973.[4] The value of imports was about $11 million in 1955, gradually increasing to about $60 million in 1962. Then, in the years 1963–1973, the absolute value of imports increased meteorically; in 1973 the total value was $976 million, about eleven times as much as in 1963. Note, however, that according to one estimate, one-third of the imports come from American companies operating abroad or foreign companies controlled by American interests [60].

Although Italy continues to maintain its position as the leading exporter of footwear in value terms, its share in the total United States imports declined from 49.6% in 1963 to 37% in 1973. The overall decline indicates successful inroads made by other exporting countries, especially Brazil and Taiwan. The latter's share in United States footwear imports climbed in 1973 to 35.4% measured in physical terms and 11.9% in dollar terms. On the other hand, we are witnessing the gradual disappearance of Japan as a footwear exporter to the United States. In 1973 three leading countries—Italy, Spain, and Taiwan— accounted for about 68.3% of the total value of American footwear imports. The next three countries, Brazil, France, and West Germany, accounted for about 12% of the total value of imports.

An examination of the import pattern reveals that the percentage increase in footwear imports from North and South America (particularly, Brazil) was the highest of the four major exporting areas (the other three are Europe, Asia, and other countries), registering over a fortyfold increase since 1963. As a result of this impressive growth, the share of North and South America in the United States footwear imports rose from 3.4% in 1963 to 13.1% in 1973.

Imports have been highly concentrated in women's and misses' footwear, low-priced footwear, and footwear made of vinyl. Appendix Tables I-E and I-F show imports as a percentage of market supply by footwear categories for the 1963–1973 period and average price of

---

[4]Prior to 1963 footwear imports constituted a negligible share of domestic consumption.

TABLE I-3

United States Imports of Nonrubber Footwear by Main Trading
Areas in Selected Years (Thousand Dollars)

Area	1963	1967	1970	1973
North and South America	3029	7123	25,046	127,877
Europe	66,464	164,024	414,375	651,160
Asia	16,756	40,361	98,746	154,042
Other	3296	6087	21,180	43,026
Canada	2297	4175	10,434	15,850
Mexico	732	2746	8486	14,048
United Kingdom	9187	11,449	19,478	9888
France	3069	7033	14,681	21,930
West Germany	1850	5199	16,044	17,477
Austria	1761	2689	4253	16,598
Czechoslovakia	399	4449	4410	5208
Switzerland	2997	5490	8718	7699
Spain	2823	22,964	78,098	189,173
Italy	44,378	102,731	263,991	360,684
Romania	[a]	1698	1231	8640
India	517	1398	2938	3090
Taiwan	[a]	3135	28,713	116,585
Hong Kong	594	1091	3970	4622
Japan	15,645	34,231	60,182	12,929
Korean Republic	[a]	506	2943	16,816
Brazil	[a]	202	6126	81,260
Greece	[a]	322	3471	13,863
Argentina	[a]	[a]	[a]	16,719
Other countries	3296	6087	21,180	43,026
Grand total	89,545	217,595	559,347	976,105

[a]Small quantities included with Other countries.
SOURCE: American Footwear Industry Association [75, p. 84].

imports by types and country for 1973. These trends are also shown in
Figure I-2.

During the early 1970s the United States absorbed approximately
the following shares of total national footwear exports: Brazil, 90%;
Taiwan, 80%; Spain, 70%; and Italy, 40%.

From 1963 to 1973 imports increased by $886.6 million. The Euro-
pean markets contributed the most to this increase, accounting for 66%
of the total increase. The rates of contribution of the other three
principal regions to the increase in the value of footwear imports during

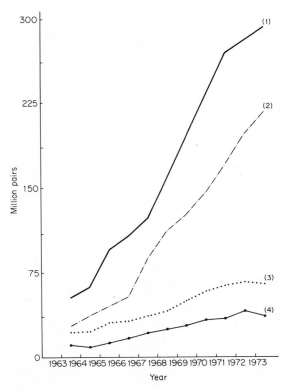

Figure I-2. United States imports of leather and vinyl footwear, 1963–1973. LEGEND: (1) total nonrubber; (2) women's shoes; (3) men's shoes; (4) children's and infants' shoes.

the same period were 15.5% for Asia; 14.1% for North and South America; and 4.5% for the other countries.

3. SIZE DISTRIBUTION OF FIRMS

The number and size distribution of firms in an industry is relevant to the question of the character, intensity of competition, and determination of the market category into which the industry falls. Markets characterized by insignificant concentration fulfill one of the requirements for effective competition, namely large numbers of sellers providing many alternatives to buyers. In other words, the size distribution of firms provides a measure of the ability or inability of individual firms to exercise market power.

A variety of indexes to measure concentration exist.[5] Number of employees, total assets, sales or physical output, and value added by manufacture offer four possible measuring rods. For our purposes, the volume of employment would serve as a good indicator of size, since the industrial units throughout the industry employ almost identical equipment and there has been little change in production techniques. In some instances, the availability of data dictates the use of value of shipments—proxy variable for dollar sales—as another dimension of size.[6]

Trend

Table I-4 presents the cumulative percentage distribution of establishments and persons engaged for the years 1954, 1958, 1963, 1967, and 1972. Over this period, the distribution indicates the relative stability of the median size groups with respect to both the number of establishments (100–249 persons engaged) and the number of persons engaged (250–499 persons engaged). However, some changes have occurred in the tails of the distribution.

In the smaller size classes (1–49 employees), the share of establishments in 1972 is 4 percentage points smaller than in 1954, whereas that of employees was smaller by about 1 percentage point, an indication of the tendency of those plants to become larger. At the upper levels of the size distribution, we find no plants with more than 2500 employees in 1972. In 1954, there was one such plant.

In the larger size classes, establishments employing 250 or more employees, we find no change in the proportion of plants in 1972 compared with 1954, but the number of employees in those plants has increased by 4 percentage points. This suggests some increase in the size of firm and the degree of concentration within those firms.

---

[5]A critical evaluation of concentration measurements is found in Adelman [30], reprinted in Stocking and Heflebower [39]. Also see Rosenbluth [65].

[6]The use of employment as an indicator of size is less fully satisfactory whenever it is affected by differences in capital intensity in production, worker productivity, length of workday and workweek, and the utilization of plant. Value of shipments may be an unsatisfactory basis for measurement whenever heavy shipments between establishments occur, leading to duplication.

TABLE I-4

Absolute and Cumulative Percentage Distribution of Establishments and Persons Engaged in the Footwear Industry, 1954, 1958, 1963, 1967, 1972

Size group (by number of persons engaged)	1954 Establishments		1954 Persons engaged		1958 Establishments		1958 Persons engaged	
	Number	Cumulative percent of total	Number	Cumulative percent of total	Number	Cumulative percent of total	Number	Cumulative percent of total
1–49	419	35.1	7046	3.2	350	31.4	5521	2.6
50–99	144	47.1	10,623	8.1	118	42.0	8479	6.5
100–249	286	71.0	48,279	30.1	282	67.3	46,470	28.1
250–499	266	93.2	93,229	72.6	296	93.8	103,852	76.4
500–999	71	99.1	45,775	93.4	63	99.5	41,083	95.5
1000–2499	9	99.9	14,419	100.0	5	99.9	9846	100.0
2500 and over	1	100.0	a		1	100.0	a	
Total	1196		219,375		1115		215,311	

Size group (by number of persons engaged)	1963 Establishments		1963 Persons engaged		1967 Establishments		1967 Persons engaged	
	Number	Cumulative percent of total	Number	Cumulative percent of total	Number	Cumulative percent of total	Number	Cumulative percent of total
1–49	335	32.2	4822	2.4	284	29.8	3600	1.8
50–99	104	42.2	7975	6.3	94	39.7	7300	5.5
100–249	247	66.0	41,678	27.0	220	62.8	37,700	24.5
250–499	288	93.7	101,685	77.4	283	92.6	100,600	75.2
500–999	62	99.7	38,456	96.5	63	99.2	40,100	95.4
1000–2499	3	99.9	7112	100.0	7	100.0	9400	100.0
2500 and over	1	100.0	a					
Total	1040		201,728		951		198,700	

TABLE I-4 (*Continued*)

Size group (by number of persons engaged)	1954				1958			
	Establishments		Persons engaged		Establishments		Persons engaged	
	Number	Cumulative percent of total	Number	Cumulative percent of total	Number	Cumulative percent of total	Number	Cumulative percent of total
1972								
1–49	256	31.0	3500	2.1				
50–99	75	40.1	5500	5.4				
100–249	200	64.3	33,800	25.5				
250–499	240	93.4	86,400	77.0				
500–999	50	99.5	38,600	100.0				
1000–2499	5	100.0	a					
2500 and over								
Total	826		167,800					

aWithheld to avoid disclosing figures for individual companies. Employment figure included in previous class.

SOURCE: United States Bureau of the Census, *Census of Manufactures* (various years).

Men's and Women's Footwear Manufacturing

The foregoing discussion includes plants manufacturing all categories of footwear. The 1972 Census of Manufactures overcomes, in part, this shortcoming in that it establishes three more homogeneous subclasses. These may be identified as men's footwear (except athletic), footwear for women (except athletic), and footwear except rubber NEC (see Table I-5).

The most striking feature of the comparison between the first two categories is the pronounced difference at both ends of the distributions. As far as the largest establishments are concerned—defined as plants employing 500 or more workers—men's footwear plants engage twice the proportion of employees (about 35%) than those for women's footwear. In the smallest size class—defined as plants employing up to 49 employees—one finds the exact opposite to be true. Here, the companies manufacturing women's footwear engage 2.6% of total sub-industry employment, whereas those for men's footwear employ 1.3%. Furthermore, the scale of operations for the manufacturing of men's shoes exceeds by far that for women's footwear, as evidenced by the average employment per plant and higher concentration ratios. (See Appendix Table I-G.) For men's footwear, it stands at 278 employees per plant as compared with 183 for women's footwear. What accounts for this development is that men's shoes are conducive to more uniform or standardized operations. In the case of women's shoes, more frequent changes in response to the dictates of fashion, greater variety of styles, and considerable range of products provide an environment in which smaller plants can operate efficiently.

Concentration Ratios

The data in Table I-6 list the concentrations of shipments among the leading four, eight, twenty, and fifty establishments for nonrubber shoes and slippers, and provide evidence of the insignificant changes that occurred in these ratios. The changes in the concentration ratios for the four and eight largest shoe-producing companies were in the opposite direction as for the largest twenty and fifty companies between 1954 and 1967. In the house slippers segment of the industry, the movement of the concentration ratios among the top companies was in the same direction.

TABLE 1-5

Distribution of Footwear Industry Employment in Men's Except Athletic, Women's Except Athletic, and Footwear Except Rubber NEC,[a] 1972

Men's footwear except athletic

Class size	Number of plants	Percent of total	Employment	Percent of total
1–49	44	19.9	800	1.3
50–99	12	5.4	800	1.3
100–249	56	25.4	9500	15.4
250–499	79	35.7	29,100	47.2
500 and over	30	13.6	21,400	34.7
Total	221	100.0	61,600	100.0

Women's footwear except athletic

Class size	Number of plants	Percent of total	Employment	Percent of total
1–49	145	34.4	2000	2.6
50–99	45	10.7	3300	4.3
100–249	94	22.3	16,000	20.6
250–499	118	28.0	42,600	54.5
500 and over	20	4.7	13,700	17.7
Total	422	100.0	77,600	100.0

Footwear except rubber NEC

Class size	Number of plants	Percent of total	Employment	Percent of total
1–49	67	36.6	700	2.4
50–99	18	9.8	1400	4.9
100–249	50	27.3	8300	29.0
250–499	43	23.5	14,700	51.4
500 and over	5	2.7	3500	12.2
Total	183	100.0	28,600	100.0

[a]Not elsewhere classified.

SOURCE: United States Department of Commerce, Bureau of the Census, *Census of Manufactures* (1972); *Current Industrial Reports* "Tanning, Industrial Leather Goods and Shoes," MC72(2)-31A (1975).

TABLE I-6

Concentration Ratios for Nonrubber Footwear

Industry SIC[a] code and classification	Year	Number of companies	Value of shipments (million dollars)	Concentration ratios (percent of total value of shipments)			
				Four largest firms	Eight largest firms	Twenty largest firms	Fifty largest firms
3141: shoes except rubber	1954	970	1790	30	36	45	b
	1958	871	2026	27	34	43	55
	1963	784	2249	25	32	43	57
	1967	676	2780	27	34	46	61
	1970	b	1658	28	36	b	b
3142: house slippers	1954	170	90	19	31	54	b
	1958	159	111	18	30	56	83
	1963	149	123	20	34	58	84
	1967	125	181	22	37	63	88
	1970	b	b	28	44	b	b

[a]Standard industrial classification.
[b]Not available.
SOURCE: United States Bureau of the Census, *Census of Manufactures* (1967).

13

In 1954 the top twenty shoe-producing companies accounted for 45% of total shipments. By 1958 this figure declined to 43%. It remained the same in 1963 and rose to 46% in 1967. For house slippers, the ratio for the fifty top firms increased from 83% in 1958 to 88% in 1967. The ratios for the four largest companies fell slightly, while those for house slippers increased somewhat over the period 1954–1970.[7] (See also Appendix Table I-H.)

A summary index of employment concentration is the Gini coefficient, which takes into account the entire number and size distribution of firms in the industry. This is possible for the census years.[8] The coefficient, based on the Lorenz curve, relates the percentage of total employment (or any other indicator of size) to the percentage of firms in the market, cumulated from the smallest to the largest.[9] An industry composed of firms identical in size has a curve that coincides with a line OZ, which is referred to as the diagonal of equal distribution. The Gini coefficient in such a case assumes a value of zero. At the other extreme, where one firm accounts for all employment in the industry, the area of concentration coincides with the area under the diagonal of equal distribution, and the coefficient equals unity. If the firms are unequal in size, there will be a divergence between the theoretical diagonal of equal distribution and the actually observed distribution. The greater the disparity between sizes of the largest and the smallest firms, the greater the resulting degree of concentration.[10]

The data in Appendix Table I-J, which show the pertinent computations of the Gini coefficients for the years 1954, 1958, 1963, 1967, and 1972, indicate a slight movement toward deconcentration until 1958 and its stability after that year. Between 1954 and 1958 the coefficient declined from 0.54 to 0.51, and thereafter it did not change. These findings are also shown for selected years in Figure I-3.

---

[7]Concentration ratios compiled by the American Footwear Manufacturers Association (AFMA) between 1954 and 1966 for the four, eight, and fifty top footwear producers, using physical production as the dimension of size, exhibit similar trends.

[8]The concentration ratios consider only the top size classes.

[9]For an evaluation of the technique using the Lorenz curve and the Gini coefficient see Blair [48, pp. 355–356], Hart and Prais (54, pp. 150–181], Adelman [40, pp. 68–69], and Prais [63, p. 268].

[10]The Gini coefficient is applied in Horowitz and Horowitz [55, pp. 129–153], Kemp [29], and Lombardi [7].

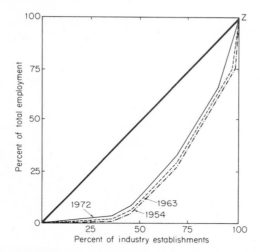

Figure I-3. Lorenz diagram showing the degree of concentration in the American footwear industry, 1954, 1963, and 1972.

4. STRUCTURE OF DISTRIBUTION CHANNELS

The footwear industry's concentration at the production level does not represent a significant departure from a highly competitive structure. However, attention must be directed toward the structure of the market at the distribution level. If this function is served by a few wholesalers, an element of oligopsonistic market power may affect the performance of the footwear industry.

The variety of retailing establishments—over 110,000 retail outlets owned by some 80,000 different firms—is no evidence of the wide range of choice of distributive outlets available to the independent single footwear manufacturer.

Maintenance of a distributive outlet represents a substantial investment and requires the ability to offer a wide variety of styles and categories of footwear. In general, the greater the variety and range offered, the greater is the chance of securing high margins, since the seller is able to follow changes in demand. This can be accomplished only by a large manufacturer or a large distributor who has the financial resources to stock shoes whenever market conditions warrant.

A small manufacturing plant unable to meet these requirements must either rely on wholesalers in locating retailers or utilize the services of large establishments to dispose of its small output—very frequently at reduced prices. The small manufacturer is thus put at a disadvantage, since this increases marketing costs and represents a moderate barrier to entry. The marketing aspect represents the main force behind the growing trend toward integration of manufacturing and retailing interests [32, pp. 26–28].[11]

Other, more general, factors account as well for the integrative tendencies. These are the growth of media for reaching mass markets economically and the rapid rate of urbanization (and suburbanization) that has increased the density of the principal consumer markets. Also, as scale economies in marketing and retailing become increasingly important,[12] the ability of retail chains to compete for premium value sites is enhanced. Table I-7 shows the distribution of footwear by two major types of retail outlets. The trend for independents and retail chains reveals that the independents' share has steadily but gradually declined. In 1963 they accounted for 51.4% of sales, while in 1971 the figure declined to 45.9%. Table I-8 shows footwear sales by types of retail outlets. Sales by firms composed of ten or fewer units rose by only 30%, while department store sales increased by more than 125%, and sales by chain stores by 112%.

5. SUMMARY

Total American imports expanded sharply in the late 1960s. In 1960 only 5% of all footwear purchased in this country was imported, and only 2% in value terms. In 1973 the shares reached 40% and 22%, respectively. Since consumption did not rise at as rapid a rate, the period beginning with 1968 was marked by declining domestic production. In broad terms, the United States imports from two groups of countries: (1) Far Eastern suppliers, which produce low-value products largely made of vinyl, and (2) European and Brazilian producers, which specialize in higher-value leather footwear.

[11]Unfortunately, the paucity of data does not enable us to document these statements.

[12]The growth of regional and national chains in such related fields as food, clothing, and many other consumer goods is evidence of this trend. See also *Wall Street Journal* [72].

TABLE I-7

United States Footwear Distribution by Major
Type of Retail Outlet[a]

	Total		Independents		Chains	
Year	Sales (thousand dollars)	Percent of sales	Sales (thousand dollars)	Percent of total	Sales (thousand dollars)	Percent of total
1963	4,199,127	100.0	2,156,296	51.4	2,042,831	48.6
1967	5,341,065	100.0	2,556,925	47.9	2,784,140	52.1
1971	6,850,450	100.0	3,143,997	45.9	3,706,453	54.1

[a]Stores with payrolls only.
SOURCE: American Footwear Industry Association [75, p. 162].

TABLE I-8

Estimated Sales of Footwear by Type of Retail Outlet,
1958, 1963, 1968 (Million Dollars)

Outlet	1958	1963	1968	Percent change 1958–1968	Share of market	
					1963	1968
Shoe stores, total	2130	2390	3290	54.5	49.4	50.6
Under 11 units	1240	1328	1690	36.3	27.4	26.0
11–100 units	188	246	377	100.0	5.1	5.8
101 and over units	702	816	1223	74.2	16.9	18.8
Department stores, total	670	1084	1520	126.9	22.4	23.4
Under 11 units	257	321	340	32.3	6.6	5.2
11–100 units	196	407	596	204.0	8.4	9.2
101 and over units	216	357	584	170.4	7.4	9.0
Family clothing stores, total	348	404	460	32.2	8.4	7.1
Under 11 units	248	268	275	10.9	5.5	4.2
11–100 units	62	59	55	−11.3	1.2	0.8
101 and over units	38	77	130	242.1	1.6	2.0
All other[a]	626	786	960	126.0	16.2	14.8
Under 11 units	405	437	480	19.0	9.0	7.4
11 and over units	221	349	480	107.0	7.2	7.4
Mail order catalog	113	133	170	50.4	2.7	2.6
All other kinds	189	42	100	−47.1	0.9	1.5
Total market	4075	4838	6500	59.5	100.0	100.0

[a]Includes women's ready to wear, men's and boys' ready to wear, general merchandise, and limited price variety.
SOURCE: *Report of the Task Force on Nonrubber Footwear* [38, p. 100].

The domestic footwear industry still has a highly competitive structure at the production level, with a gradually evolving oligopolistic/oligopsonistic one at the distribution end. However, the latter is attenuated by the increasing role of imports. Examination of the change in the industry's structure has shown two main kinds of development: First, the industry has experienced a decline in both the number of plants and employment, with the largest employment decline recorded by the smallest size class. Second, the scale of operations for manufacturing of men's shoes exceeds by far that for women's shoes and for all other footwear.

We find the industry to be imbued with a competitive and individualistic spirit, which is reflected in the absence of restrictive agreements among firms and the infrequency of mergers.

APPENDIX TO CHAPTER I

Tables I-A through I-J appear on the following pages.

TABLE I-A

United States Imports of Nonrubber Footwear by Main Trading Areas, 1963–1973 (Thousand Dollars)

Area	1963	1964	1965	1966	1967	1968	1969	1970	1971	1972	1973
North and South America	3029	2825	3158	4377	7123	9723	13,471	25,046	44,067	65,030	127,877
Europe	66,464	76,857	87,651	116,103	164,024	251,693	332,965	414,375	485,695	593,361	651,160
Asia	16,756	20,865	23,231	27,969	40,361	59,468	77,525	98,746	129,022	142,162	154,042
Other	3296	3126	4438	5119	6087	7387	11,923	21,180	19,568	34,432	43,026
Canada	2297	2112	2435	2932	4175	5213	6878	10,434	10,006	11,377	15,850
Mexico	732	713	723	1445	2746	4301	5182	8486	9585	9791	14,048
United Kingdom	9187	8948	9080	10,273	11,449	16,145	20,836	19,478	17,624	13,580	9888
France	3069	3931	4956	5584	7033	8082	9419	14,681	16,307	17,813	21,930
West Germany	1850	2419	3135	3997	5199	6602	11,005	16,044	16,921	19,303	17,477
Austria	1761	2406	2869	2688	2689	2815	3700	4253	4071	7687	16,598
Czechoslovakia	399	1381	2312	3443	4449	4260	5728	4410	4418	5148	5208
Switzerland	2997	3487	4458	4752	5490	7076	8290	8718	8986	9316	7699
Spain	2823	4116	6519	10,269	22,964	47,614	73,468	78,098	125,275	171,431	189,173
Italy	44,378	50,169	54,044	74,361	102,731	157,054	197,128	263,991	285,152	337,262	360,684
Romania	a	a	278	736	1698	1409	1349	1231	1804	2862	8640
India	517	478	671	1096	1398	2014	2109	2938	3191	3845	3090
Taiwan	a	a	245	1109	3135	7795	14,249	28,713	50,352	79,331	116,585
Hong Kong	594	772	533	521	1091	1824	2765	3970	4959	4773	4622
Japan	15,645	19,615	21,782	25,243	34,231	46,926	57,244	60,182	64,466	40,800	12,929
Korean Republic	a	a	a	a	506	909	1158	2943	6054	13,413	16,816
Brazil	a	a	a	a	202	209	1191	6126	23,405	41,806	81,260
Greece	a	a	a	a	322	636	2042	3471	5137	8959	13,863
Argentina	a	a	a	a	a	a	220	a	1071	2056	16,719
Other countries	3296	3126	4438	5119	6087	7387	11,923	21,180	19,568	34,432	43,026
Grand total	89,454	103,674	118,478	158,569	217,595	328,272	435,884	559,347	678,352	834,985	976,105

a Small quantities included with other countries.

SOURCE: American Footwear Industry Association [75, p. 84].

19

TABLE I-B

Percentage Distribution of Nonrubber Footwear Imports by Main Trading Areas, 1963–1973 (Dollars)

Area	1963	1964	1965	1966	1967	1968	1969	1970	1971	1972	1973
North and South America	3.4	2.7	2.7	2.8	3.3	3.0	3.1	4.5	6.5	7.8	13.1
Europe	74.2	74.1	74.0	73.2	75.4	76.7	76.4	74.1	71.6	71.1	66.7
Asia	18.7	20.1	19.6	17.6	18.5	18.1	17.8	17.7	19.0	17.0	15.8
Canada	2.6	2.0	2.1	1.8	1.9	1.6	1.6	1.9	1.5	1.4	1.6
Mexico	0.8	0.7	0.6	0.9	1.3	1.3	1.2	1.5	1.4	1.2	1.4
United Kingdom	10.3	8.6	7.7	6.5	5.3	4.9	4.8	3.5	2.6	1.6	1.0
France	3.4	3.8	4.2	3.5	3.2	2.5	2.2	2.6	2.4	2.1	2.2
West Germany	2.1	2.4	2.6	2.5	2.4	2.0	2.5	2.9	2.5	2.3	1.8
Austria	2.0	2.3	2.4	1.7	1.2	0.9	0.8	0.8	0.6	0.9	1.7
Czechoslovakia	0.4	1.3	2.0	2.2	2.0	1.3	1.3	0.8	0.7	0.6	0.5
Switzerland	3.3	3.4	3.8	3.0	2.5	2.2	1.9	1.6	1.3	1.1	0.8
Spain	3.2	4.0	5.5	6.5	10.6	14.5	16.9	14.0	18.5	20.5	19.4
Italy	49.6	48.4	46.5	46.9	47.2	47.8	45.2	47.2	42.0	40.4	37.0
Romania	[a]	[a]	0.2	0.5	0.8	0.4	0.3	0.2	0.3	0.3	0.9
India	0.6	0.5	0.6	0.7	0.6	0.6	0.5	0.5	0.5	0.5	0.3
Taiwan	[a]	[a]	0.2	0.7	1.4	2.4	3.3	5.1	7.4	9.5	11.9
Hong Kong	0.7	0.7	0.4	0.3	0.5	0.6	0.6	0.7	0.7	0.6	0.5
Japan	17.5	18.9	18.4	15.9	15.7	14.3	13.1	10.8	9.5	4.9	1.3
Korean Republic	[a]	[a]	[a]	[a]	0.2	0.3	0.3	0.5	0.9	1.6	1.7
Brazil	[a]	[a]	[a]	[a]	0.1	0.1	0.3	1.1	3.5	5.0	8.3
Greece	[a]	[a]	[a]	[a]	0.1	0.2	0.5	0.6	0.8	1.1	1.4
Argentina	[a]	[a]	[a]	[a]	[a]	[a]	0.1	[a]	0.2	0.2	1.7
Other countries	3.7	3.0	3.7	3.2	2.8	2.3	2.7	3.8	2.9	4.1	4.4
Absolute value	89,545	103,674	118,478	158,569	217,595	328,272	435,884	559,347	678,352	834,985	976,105

[a]Small quantities included with Other countries.

SOURCE: American Footwear Industry Association [75, p. 84].

20

TABLE 1-C

United States Imports of Nonrubber Footwear by Main Trading Areas, 1963–1973 (Thousand Pairs)

Area	1963	1964	1965	1966	1967	1968	1969	1970	1971	1972	1973
North and South America	1392	1438	1381	2025	3488	4199	4806	8900	14,169	18,590	40,878
Europe	23,789	28,166	31,476	42,123	56,708	83,063	93,445	114,303	120,768	132,681	128,962
Asia	36,048	44,279	52,571	50,076	66,670	85,379	98,937	112,149	128,478	137,071	137,273
Other	1591	1489	2202	1914	2271	2651	3745	6208	5154	8323	8401
Canada	786	812	885	885	1265	1731	1978	2527	2194	2272	2665
Mexico	606	626	496	1140	1972	2468	2451	3963	3538	4044	14,810
United Kingdom	1805	1662	1599	1684	1793	2775	3144	2774	2327	1603	1063
France	1037	1187	1525	1944	2418	2622	2520	3102	2883	2957	2742
West Germany	254	303	388	546	823	962	1942	2807	2453	2660	1794
Austria	141	169	188	146	143	149	199	270	365	1373	3108
Czechoslovakia	285	931	1368	1726	1977	2036	2622	1791	1605	1928	1343
Switzerland	279	290	354	365	383	535	605	564	613	559	406
Spain	996	1491	2474	3470	6695	14,248	20,729	21,250	31,216	39,254	36,805
Italy	18,992	22,133	23,396	31,773	41,555	58,996	61,083	80,680	77,849	79,698	76,853
Romania	a	a	184	469	921	740	601	585	681	1068	2467
India	573	464	660	1050	1385	1924	2097	2926	3029	3547	2762
Taiwan	a	a	6003	2907	6715	15,316	25,897	42,045	64,787	91,259	111,702
Hong Kong	1236	1386	925	1023	1392	2300	4311	5465	5995	6813	6512
Japan	34,239	42,429	44,983	45,096	56,768	65,145	66,632	59,789	51,371	27,502	9124
Korean Republic	a	a	a	a	410	694	879	1924	3296	7950	7173
Brazil	a	a	a	a	251	a	377	2410	8136	11,809	19,528
Greece	a	a	a	a	a	a	228	480	776	1581	2381
Argentina	a	a	a	a	a	a	a	a	301	465	3875
Other countries	1591	1489	2202	1914	2271	2651	3745	6208	5154	8323	8401
Grand total	62,820	75,372	87,632	96,135	129,137	175,292	202,040	241,560	268,569	296,665	315,514

a Small quantities included with Other countries.
SOURCE: American Footwear Industry Association [75, p. 77].

TABLE 1-D

Percentage Distribution of Nonrubber Footwear Imports by Main Trading Areas, 1963–1973 (Pairs)

Area	1963	1964	1965	1966	1967	1968	1969	1970	1971	1972	1973
North and South America	3.0	1.9	1.6	2.1	2.7	2.4	2.4	3.7	5.3	6.3	12.8
Europe	37.9	37.4	35.9	43.8	43.9	47.4	46.3	47.3	45.0	44.7	41.0
Asia	57.4	58.7	60.0	52.1	51.6	48.7	49.0	46.4	47.8	46.2	43.5
Other	2.5	2.0	2.5	2.0	1.6	1.5	1.9	2.6	1.9	2.8	2.7
Canada	1.3	1.1	1.0	0.9	1.0	1.0	1.0	1.0	0.8	0.8	0.8
Mexico	1.0	0.8	0.6	1.2	1.5	1.4	1.2	1.6	1.3	1.4	4.7
United Kingdom	2.9	2.2	1.8	1.8	1.4	1.6	1.6	1.1	0.9	0.5	0.3
France	1.7	1.6	1.7	2.0	1.9	1.5	1.2	1.3	1.1	1.0	0.9
West Germany	0.4	0.4	0.4	0.6	0.6	0.5	1.0	1.2	0.9	0.9	0.6
Austria	0.2	0.2	0.2	0.2	0.1	0.1	0.1	0.1	0.1	0.5	1.0
Czechoslovakia	0.6	1.2	1.6	1.8	1.5	1.2	1.3	0.7	0.6	0.6	0.4
Switzerland	0.4	0.4	0.4	0.4	0.3	0.3	0.3	0.2	0.2	0.2	0.1
Spain	1.6	2.0	2.8	3.6	5.2	8.1	10.3	8.8	11.6	13.2	11.7
Italy	30.2	29.4	26.7	33.1	32.2	33.7	32.2	34.0	29.0	26.9	24.4
Romania	a	a	0.2	0.5	0.7	0.4	0.3	0.2	0.3	0.4	0.8
India	0.9	a	0.8	1.1	1.1	1.1	1.0	1.2	1.1	1.2	0.9
Taiwan	a	a	6.9	3.0	5.2	8.7	12.8	17.4	24.1	30.8	35.4
Hong Kong	2.0	1.8	1.1	1.1	1.1	1.3	2.1	2.3	2.2	2.3	2.1
Japan	54.5	56.3	51.3	46.9	44.0	37.2	33.0	24.8	19.1	9.3	2.9
Korean Republic	a	a	a	a	0.3	0.4	0.4	0.8	1.2	2.7	2.3
Brazil	a	a	a	a	0.2	a	0.2	1.0	3.0	4.0	6.2
Greece	a	a	a	a	a	a	0.1	0.2	0.3	0.5	0.7
Argentina	a	a	a	a	a	a	a	a	0.1	0.1	1.2
Other countries	2.5	2.0	2.5	2.0	1.6	1.5	1.9	2.6	1.9	2.8	2.7
Total	100.0	100.0	100.0	100.0	100.0	100.0	100.0	100.0	100.0	100.0	100.0

[a]Small quantities included with Other countries.

SOURCE: American Footwear Industry Association [75, p. 77].

22

TABLE I-E

United States Footwear Imports as a Percentage
of Market Supply by Categories (Pairs)

Year	Men's leather and vinyl	Youths' and boys' leather and vinyl	Men's, youths', and boys' vinyl only	Womens' leather and vinyl	Misses' leather and vinyl	Womens' and misses' vinyl only	Children's leather and vinyl
1963	10.1	5.9	*a*	12.1	3.0	*a*	3.5
1964	10.1	5.9	3.9	15.5	3.9	7.7	7.0
1965	11.4	7.2	4.8	15.7	3.9	8.0	6.9
1966	11.1	8.2	3.5	18.3	6.3	8.6	8.7
1967	13.7	10.6	3.8	25.9	10.4	13.1	13.3
1968	17.1	13.3	4.3	30.5	13.8	15.4	18.2
1969	22.3	16.3	5.4	35.3	16.1	17.6	26.7
1970	25.7	20.1	8.5	39.8	22.1	18.7	31.5
1971	29.1	25.6	10.5	43.8	33.0	21.4	29.1
1972	29.0	25.6	9.9	47.3	34.9	22.1	35.4
1973	31.4	27.7	8.8	52.2	41.5	25.0	34.2

Year	Infants' and babies' leather and vinyl	Children's, infants', and babies' vinyl only	Athletic	Slippers	Other	Total
1963	4.0	*a*	*a*	8.7	*a*	9.4
1964	7.9	1.9	*a*	4.9	*a*	11.0
1965	9.5	3.9	13.6	8.7	28.2	12.3
1966	8.6	6.2	14.1	3.7	25.6	13.0
1967	8.5	8.1	16.9	3.1	31.0	17.7
1968	8.3	9.0	17.0	2.7	40.0	21.4
1969	9.9	11.7	21.7	2.0	74.5[b]	25.9
1970	9.0	11.9	31.8	1.9	72.7	30.0
1971	16.3	12.3	39.6	1.7	80.6	33.4
1972	27.5	17.0	41.6	1.7	90.2	36.0
1973	25.9	17.2	38.0	1.5	92.1	39.3

[a]Not available.

[b]Not comparable to previous years due to inclusion of footwear NEC upper 90% rubber/plastic not shown in earlier years.

SOURCE: Computed from Tables I-A–I-D and American Footwear Industry Association [75, p. 106].

TABLE I-F

United States Imports of Footwear (Except Rubber) by Types
and Country, 1973 (Thousand Pairs; Thousand Dollars)

Country	Total[a]	Leather footwear				Other nonrubber types[c]
		Men's and boys'	Women's and misses'	Children's and infants'	All other leather types[b]	
Canada						
Pairs	2665	601	187	4	432	606
Value	15,850	7000	1566	33	3051	1641
Average[d]	5.95	11.65	8.38	8.42	7.06	2.71
Mexico						
Pairs	14,810	767	1435	52	256	11,851
Value	14,048	6055	3990	125	885	2225
Average[d]	0.95	7.89	2.78	2.42	3.46	0.19
United Kingdom						
Pairs	1063	682	144	14	40	83
Value	9885	6916	1472	92	356	345
Average[d]	9.30	10.14	10.20	6.68	8.90	4.15
France						
Pairs	2742	1884	428	14	8	250
Value	21,930	13,895	4526	73	145	1054
Average[d]	8.00	7.37	10.58	5.25	18.12	4.22
West Germany						
Pairs	1794	1355	114	32	105	107
Value	17,477	12,275	923	168	1336	336
Average[d]	9.74	9.06	8.13	5.26	12.72	3.14
Czechoslovakia						
Pairs	1343	1074	1	178	90	—
Value	5208	4308	2	418	479	—
Average[d]	3.88	4.01	2.31	2.35	5.30	—
India						
Pairs	2762	637	1788	336	e	1
Value	3090	764	1980	344	1	1
Average[d]	1.12	1.20	1.11	1.02	2.60	1.34
Hong Kong						
Pairs	6511	120	30	10	1	637
Value	4622	471	95	5	1	620
Average[d]	0.71	3.94	3.11	0.49	1.03	0.97

[a]Certain minor categories (vinyl supported uppers, vinyl 90% uppers rubber/plastic) were excluded. As a result, the sum of the categories does not add up to total.

[b]Includes welt footwear (2.9 million pairs), footwear of molded soles laced to uppers, McKay sewed footwear, leather slippers, huaraches, and moccasins.

24

TABLE I-F *(Continued)*

| Country | Total | Leather Footwear | | | | Other nonrubber types[c] |
		Men's and boys'	Women's and misses'	Children's and infants'	All other leather types[b]	
Taiwan						
Pairs	111,702	914	531	42	175	5617
Value	116,585	3040	1075	69	685	5645
Average[d]	1.04	3.33	2.03	1.65	3.91	1.00
Japan						
Pairs	9124	823	69	24	2	3812
Value	12,929	4887	226	49	9	1586
Average[d]	1.42	5.94	3.26	2.02	3.94	0.42
Spain						
Pairs	36,805	10,212	17,985	2464	91	558
Value	189,173	60,988	101,257	5833	668	2123
Average[d]	5.14	5.97	5.63	2.37	7.32	3.80
Italy						
Pairs	76,853	11,179	45,221	1957	99	2500
Value	360,684	92,113	198,475	4571	1666	7072
Average[d]	4.69	8.24	4.39	2.34	16.83	2.83
Korean Republic						
Pairs	7173	1080	2	15	810	1777
Value	16,816	5444	10	35	4446	2054
Average[d]	2.34	5.04	5.10	2.37	5.49	1.16
Brazil						
Pairs	19,528	3801	14,513	543	37	405
Value	81,260	25,012	53,095	1127	268	997
Average[d]	4.16	6.58	3.66	2.07	7.26	2.46
Argentina						
Pairs	3875	888	2711	40	1	232
Value	16,719	6343	9553	102	13	699
Average[d]	4.31	7.14	3.52	2.56	11.59	3.01
Other countries						
Pairs	16,764	5266	4295	355	1360	4066
Value	89,826	34,270	22,184	814	6398	14,320
Average[d]	5.36	6.51	5.17	2.29	4.70	3.52
Total						
Pairs	315,514	41,283	89,454	6080	3507	32,052
Value	976,105	283,781	400,429	13,858	20,407	40,718
Average[d]	3.09	6.87	4.48	2.28	5.82	1.25

[c] Includes footwear made of wool felt, textiles, vegetable fiber, or wood, and also footwear with leather soles and fiber uppers.

[d] Dollars per pair.

[e] Less than 500.

SOURCE: American Footwear Industry Association [75, p. 95].

TABLE I-F *(Continued)*

Country	Vinyl supported uppers					Country	Vinyl supported uppers			
	Men's and boys'	Women's and misses'	Children's and infants'	Vinyl 90% uppers, rubber/plastic			Men's and boys'	Women's and misses'	Children's and infants'	Vinyl 90% uppers, rubber/plastic
Canada						Japan				
Pairs	4	143	2	13		Pairs	1150	2065	871	306
Value	32	1457	3	171		Value	2509	2519	814	327
Average[a]	8.33	10.18	1.08	12.84		Average	2.18	1.22	0.93	1.07
Mexico						Spain				
Pairs	36	192	5	217		Pairs	291	3430	1344	424
Value	54	511	7	196		Value	1091	13,373	2336	1480
Average[a]	4.78	1.84	1.50	0.93		Average	3.75	3.90	1.74	3.49
United Kingdom						Italy				
Pairs	29	47	6	16		Pairs	758	12,559	323	2230
Value	288	359	6	48		Value	8443	36,805	640	10,811
Average[a]	10.09	7.60	0.94	2.96		Average	11.04	2.93	1.98	4.85
France						Korean Republic				
Pairs	20	114	7	18		Pairs	984	1883	189	352
Value	556	858	33	790		Value	1439	2579	179	553
Average[a]	27.92	7.55	4.38	43.81		Average	1.46	1.37	0.95	1.57

26

West Germany				
Pairs	42	19	[e]	18
Value	1639	343	3	433
Average[a]	38.94	17.96	14.28	24.22
Hong Kong				
Pairs	855	2105	849	1860
Value	626	1534	658	563
Average[a]	0.73	0.73	0.77	0.30
Taiwan				
Pairs	14,280	73,365	6995	9184
Value	19,472	71,794	5882	8501
Average[a]	1.36	0.98	0.84	0.93
Brazil				
Pairs	27	183	15	3
Value	20	719	15	7
Average	0.74	3.93	0.99	2.28
Other Countries				
Pairs	178	834	35	364
Value	4075	3176	40	4418
Average	22.89	3.81	1.14	12.14
Total				
Pairs	18,654	96,942	1445	15,005
Value	40,244	136,036	10,616	28,298
Average	2.16	1.40	1.00	1.89

TABLE I-G

Concentration Ratios for Men's and Women's Dress Shoes

Industry SIC code and classification	Year	Value of shipments (thousand dollars)	Concentration ratios[a]			
			Four largest firms	Eight largest firms	Twenty largest firms	Fifty largest firms
31431: men's dress	1954	438,608	[b]	[b]	[b]	[b]
shoes including	1958	472,469	39	53	70	87
play shoes	1963	531,013	38	52	71	89
	1967	669,400	37	51	72	92
	1972	714,000				
31414: women's dress,	1954	874,280				
work, and play	1958	996,402	24	32	43	59
shoes	1963	1,065,523	24	30	43	62
	1967	1,249,100	27	33	47	66
	1972	1,305,500				

[a]In percent of total value of shipments.
[b]Not available.
SOURCE: United States Bureau of the Census, *Census of Manufactures* (1967).

TABLE I-H

Concentration Ratios for Nonrubber Footwear

Year	Concentration ratios[a]		
	Four largest firms	Eight largest firms	Fifty largest firms
1954	22.8	28.4	46.0
1962	23.3	28.8	51.4
1965	21.6	28.7	53.9
1966	20.6	28.0	53.2

[a]In percent of pairs. This compilation was discontinued after 1966.
SOURCE: American Footwear Manufacturing Association (AFMA) based on data from *Boot and Shoe Recorder*, 1974.

TABLE I-J

Computation of the Gini Coefficients (G) in Census Years

	1954			1958	
(0.032)	(0.351)	= 0.011232	(0.026)	(0.314)	= 0.008164
(0.032 +	0.081)(0.120)	= 0.013560	(0.026 +	0.065)(0.106)	= 0.009646
(0.081 +	0.301)(0.239)	= 0.091298	(0.065 +	0.281)(0.253)	= 0.087538
(0.301 +	0.726)(0.222)	= 0.227994	(0.281 +	0.764)(0.265)	= 0.279925
(0.726 +	0.934)(0.059)	= 0.097940	(0.764 +	0.955)(0.057)	= 0.097983
(0.934 +	1.000)(0.009)	= <u>0.017406</u>	(0.955 +	1.000)(0.005)	= <u>0.009775</u>
		0.459430			0.493031

$G = 1 - 0.459430 = 0.54057$ $\qquad$ $G = 1 - 0.493031 = 0.508924$

	1963			1967	
(0.024)	(0.322)	= 0.007728	(0.018)	(0.298)	= 0.005364
(0.024 +	0.063)(0.100)	= 0.008700	(0.018 +	0.055)(0.099)	= 0.007227
(0.063 +	0.270)(0.238)	= 0.079254	(0.055 +	0.245)(0.231)	= 0.069300
(0.270 +	0.774)(0.277)	= 0.289188	(0.245 +	0.752)(0.298)	= 0.297106
(0.774 +	0.965)(0.060)	= 0.104340	(0.752 +	0.954)(0.066)	= 0.112596
(0.965 +	1.000)(0.003)	= <u>0.005895</u>	(0.954 +	1.000)(0.0007)	= <u>0.001368</u>
		0.495105			0.492961

$G = 1 - 0.495105 = 0.504895$ $\qquad$ $G = 1 - 0.492961 = 0.507039$

	1972	
(0.021)	(0.310)	= 0.006510
(0.021 +	0.054)(0.091)	= 0.006825
(0.054 +	0.255)(0.242)	= 0.074778
(0.255 +	0.770)(0.291)	= 0.298275
(0.770 +	1.000)(0.066)	= <u>0.116820</u>
		0.503208

$G = 1 - 0.503208 = 0.496792$

II

ESTIMATING THE ECONOMIES OF SCALE AND THE CONDITIONS OF ENTRY

1. METHODS OF ESTIMATION

Identification of the optimum establishment size is necessary to ascertain the industry's competitive posture. Our analysis rests on two kinds of evidence. The first bases its estimate of the optimum plant size on the "survivor technique." The second relates gross profit to establishment size.

Survivor Technique

The basic postulate of the survivor technique is that the size of plant with the minimum cost will tend to have a higher probability of survival in the market place than the less efficient ones. George Stigler, the modern advocate of this technique, maintains that "an efficient size of the firm is one that meets any and all problems the entrepreneur actually faces: strained labor relations, rapid innovation, government regulation, unstable foreign markets and what not. This is, of course, the decisive meaning of efficiency from the viewpoint of the enterprise" [71, p. 56]. Thomas Saving, who applied the technique to 137 industries, asserts: "If we simply find that a certain size of plant is gaining more and more of the total industry output (or input), we can say with almost complete certainty that this size of plant lies within the range of optimum size of plants" [67, p. 573].[1]

An examination of the conditions prevailing in the industry must precede any mechanical application of this technique. Only when an industry is characterized by minimal market imperfections and by most of its plants at an identical stage of technological development, will the survival technique estimates likely be valid. The nonrubber footwear industry generally appears to meet these criteria. The industry, likewise, appears to be free from the objection that the efficiency of a particular size class may be traceable to predatory or restrictive policies rather than to size. Nor does it appear that the survival quality of footwear plants reflects the paternalistic attitudes of the larger plants toward smaller ones, due to fear of strict enforcement of antitrust laws or their ability to circumvent the law in other respects.[2]

With regard to optimum plant size, data are available for the years 1954, 1958, 1963, 1967, and 1972 on a comparable basis. Table II-1 shows data on number of plants and volume of employment by five size classes. During this period, footwear employment declined about 23%. All size classes show a reduction in employment, with the largest employment decline registered by the smallest size class. Table II-1 also presents the percentage of total employment accounted for by each of five establishment size classes. Plants engaging from 250 to 499 persons consistently expanded their share of industry employment, increasing from 42.5% of total employment in 1954 to 51.5% in 1972. All other size classes experienced declines over the period of time surveyed. However, the trend, in all cases, exhibits slight reverse movements.

The survivor technique, therefore, quite vividly establishes the minimum optimal plant size as that employing 250 workers. Such an optimal plant, together with the necessary complement of machines, would produce approximately 1800–2400 pairs of Goodyear welted shoes per day. The record also demonstrates the tendency of footwear

---

[1]See also Weiss [73, pp. 246–261] and Shepherd [67, pp. 113–122].
[2]For a concise discussion of these points see Bain [43, pp. 99–104].

TABLE II-1

Distribution of the United States Footwear Industry Employment by Plant Size in Selected Years

Size class	1954 Number of plants	1954 Employment	1954 Percent of total employment	1958 Number of plants	1958 Employment	1958 Percent of total employment
1–49	419	7046	3.22	350	5521	2.59
50–99	144	10,623	4.84	118	8479	3.94
100–249	286	48,279	22.01	282	46,470	21.59
250–499	266	93,229	42.50	296	103,852	48.24
500 and over	81	60,194	27.44	69	50,929	23.66
Total	1196	219,375	100.00	1115	215,311	100.00

Size class	1963 Number of plants	1963 Employment	1963 Percent of total employment	1967 Number of plants	1967 Employment	1967 Percent of total employment
1–49	335	4822	2.38	284	3600	1.81
50–99	104	7975	3.95	94	7300	3.68
100–249	247	41,678	20.67	220	37,700	19.00
250–499	288	101,685	50.41	283	100,600	50.68
500 and over	66	45,568	22.59	70	49,500	24.94
Total	1040	201,728	100.00	951	198,500	100.0

Size class	1972 Number of plants	1972 Employment	1972 Percent of total employment	Ratio: 1972/1954 Number of plants	Ratio: 1972/1954 Employment
1–49	256	3500	2.08	0.61	0.50
50–99	75	5500	3.30	0.52	0.52
100–249	200	33,800	20.14	0.70	0.70
250–499	240	86,400	51.48	0.90	0.93
500 and over	55	38,600	23.00	0.68	0.64
Total	826	167,800	100.00	0.69	0.77

Ratio: 1972/1954 Number of plants	Ratio: 1972/1954 Employment
0.61	0.50
0.52	0.52
0.70	0.70
0.90	0.93
0.68	0.64
0.69	0.77

SOURCE: United States Department of Commerce, *Census of Manufactures* (various years).

33

establishments to adjust their plant scale toward the efficient scale of operation. In 1954 the minimum optimal size class and the two adjacent classes accounted for 92% of total employment. By 1972 the figure had risen to 95%.

Profit Test

The second major source of evidence bearing on plant scale economies is based on the relationship between increased sales and higher profits.[3] The major hypothesis to be tested is that the profit rate of the most efficient firms should, on the average, be larger than those of their competitors. As with price information, profit data in the footwear industry are almost impossible to obtain. Since most of the companies in the industry are small, few list their stock on major stock exchanges. As a result, only a handful publish annual earnings statements. Therefore, the most promising method of estimation seems to be an indirect one. That is, subtracting wages and salaries from value added of manufacture and expressing the result as a percentage of sales turnover. The resulting rate, an estimate of gross profit, serves effectively as a proxy variable. What little distortion there is probably takes the form of higher rates when computed on the basis of gross rather than net profit, since selling expenditures, advertising, etc., are not taken into account for the simple reason that no such information is published.

Estimates developed from census data reveal that the class size of companies employing 250–499 employees was the only size experiencing an average return on turnover higher than the one registered for the whole industry in every year surveyed (Table II-2), although the largest size class attained a slightly higher return in 1963.

Again, the profit data seem to support the following conclusion: The minimum optimal plant size engaged in the production of footwear appears to be one employing 250–499 workers. On the basis of information presented, there is a strong indication that the small size industrial units (those engaging 1–49 persons) may be effective competitors in the production of women's footwear.

---

[3]This approach, originally advanced by Bain, is adopted here with some modification. See Bain [42, pp. 293–324], reprinted in Bain [2, pp. 30–57].

TABLE II-2

Estimated Gross Profit in the United States Footwear Industry by Plant Size in Census Years

1958

Class size	Value of product	Value added	Total payroll	Estimated gross profit	Estimated gross profit as percent of value of production
1–49	55,517	27,899	16,878	11,021	19.8
50–99	77,414	40,986	26,994	13,992	18.1
100–249	423,199	224,403	141,832	82,571	19.5
250–499	999,947	535,251	310,397	224,854	22.5
500 and over	492,780	257,721	166,320	91,401	18.6
Total	2,048,857	1,086,260	662,421	433,839	20.7

1963

Class size	Value of product	Value added	Total payroll	Estimated gross profit	Estimated gross profit as percent of value of production
1–49	53,705	25,018	15,889	9129	17.0
50–99	85,010	44,221	27,569	16,652	19.6
100–249	422,292	225,691	144,430	81,261	19.2
250–499	1,154,730	635,816	352,065	283,751	24.6
500 and over	445,585	283,994	173,624	110,370	24.7
Total	2,249,167	1,214,740	713,577	501,163	22.3

1967

Class size	Value of product	Value added	Total payroll	Estimated gross profit	Estimated gross profit as percent of value of production
1–49	47,200	26,600	13,700	12,900	27.3
50–99	98,700	50,300	29,800	20,500	20.8
100–249	461,800	262,300	141,832	120,468	26.1
250–499	1,448,700	803,900	310,397	493,503	34.1
500 and over	713,800	382,300	166,320	215,980	30.3
Total	2,770,200	2,770,500	1,525,700	662,421	31.2

1972

Class size	Value of product	Value added	Total payroll	Estimated gross profit	Estimated gross profit as percent of value of production
1–49	57,700	31,500	19,300	12,200	21.1
50–99	85,700	48,500	28,200	20,300	23.7
100–249	544,700	298,600	173,800	124,800	22.9
250–499	1,651,400	925,900	468,600	457,300	27.8
500 and over	781,700	406,100	238,800	171,300	21.9
Total	3,120,800	1,709,900	924,700	785,200	25.2

SOURCE: United States Department of Commerce, *Census of Manufactures* (various years).

35

Technical Aspects of Footwear Production

The processes and operations used in the production of shoes vary between, as well as within, firms. The basic work flow depicted in Figure II-1 represents a general outline of these processes, though it is not meant to be comprehensive.

The first step in the production of shoes takes place in the complementary tanning industry, where the raw hides and skins are first bated, bleached, and softened in preparation for the tanning process. The tanning proper consists of soaking hide or skin in certain solutions made from vegetable materials or in biochromate of soda derived from chrome ore. The former process, used mostly on hides for soles, takes 15–45 days, while the latter, used generally on skins for uppers, takes 10–24 hr. Soles are then stuffed with hot grease, whereas the upper leathers are first dyed and then fatliquored with hot oils. The skins that are to be used in the upper shoe are then finished by a series of complex polishing, buffing, and glazing operations, which may take months to complete on a fine piece of leather. The finished leather then goes to the shoe cutstock industry to be cut into the shapes required in the fabrication of the finished shoe. This complementary industry also prepares various miscellaneous items such as laces, eyelets, tips, etc.

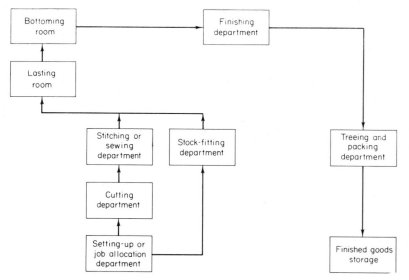

Figure II-1.   Typical work flow in a footwear factory.

The fabrication of the shoe proper is a highly complex series of over 200 mechanized operations. About 60% of the effort is directed toward getting the shoe ready to wear, and the remainder to preparing it for sale, that is, polishing it and dressing it up. Shoe factories are divided into "departments," as they are called in the industry.

The setting-up department inspects the procured leather, which if found in good condition is dispatched to the cutting department or the stock-fitting department. The cutting department cuts the upper parts of the shoe, including linings, from sheets of leather or other material. This cutting operation, also known as "clicking," may be performed by hand, in which case the clicker uses a knife to cut around a brass-rimmed, cardboard pattern, or by press, in preparation for stamp-pressing the part. Clicking is a highly specialized operation because of the variation in the quality and thickness of leather, the need to match parts of the upper, and the need to economize leather. Press cutting is estimated to be 50% faster than hand cutting, according to industry opinion. At factories where long runs of each style, color, and size are made, a clicker may work on a single style of shoe indefinitely and will draw upon large batches of leather at a time. In other factories, where fashion shoes are made, the clicker may only make a few of each style at a time, particularly toward the end of the season. After the uppers are cut, they are tied in bundles and transported to the sewing department in baskets; each basket contains all the upper parts, including linings, for the same number of shoes as are placed on one rack by the factory.

The sewing department performs all sewing operations necessary to assemble the parts into complete uppers. Skiving the edges of the uppers to reduce thickness—thus avoiding unsightly seams—is also performed in this department prior to sewing. The machines used in this operation are relatively inexpensive as compared with the labor costs involved, and they are usually purchased outright. One method of organizing work in this department, at least in the modern factory, is to use a conveyor belt to carry trays with batches of the parts to their destination. The operators are seated with their equipment (sewing or skiving machines) on either side of the conveyor belt and the supervisor controls the dispatch of trays to each operator. When an operation has been completed, the batch is returned on the conveyor and is forwarded to the appropriate operator for the next operation to be performed. Often, instead of using conveyor belts, trays of work may be carried by the operators from one station to another.

The stock-fitting department prepares the various parts of the sole for assembling, lasting, and making. The parts are bundled and transported in baskets to the lasting department. The flow of work in the stock-fitting department and in the cutting and sewing departments is so timed that the baskets of sole materials and the upper parts of each lot of shoes arrive in the lasting department together. The making department consists of the lasting and bottoming rooms.

The lasting room includes the operations by which the components of the shoe are assembled on the last and the shoe upper is drawn tightly over the last and attached to the insole. A last is a wood or plastic model of a foot. The lasting process ends when the shoe is ready to be bottomed. At the beginning of the lasting process, where the parts are assembled on the last, the shoes are placed on wheeled racks which are used to transport them from this point through to treeing and packing. A rack is a frame that resembles a bookcase on wheels, with the shelves designed to provide a separate socket for each shoe. Racks usually hold 18–36 pairs, with 6 pairs to a shelf.

The bottoming room, as the name implies, attaches the outsole to the lasted shoe, attaches and finishes the heels, finishes the sole edges, and otherwise completes the construction of the shoe. The original methods of attaching the bottoms to the uppers were nailing and stitching, but these rather crude methods have and are being superseded by the various methods of cementing and molding. Tables 10–13 of the *Footwear Manual* [75] outline the percentage breakdown of footwear produced by basic constructions and show the cemented process to be the most widely used. This is true for all footwear categories except the production of men's shoes, where the Goodyear process is still predominant.

In the finishing department, the bottom is finished off and the lasts are pulled out of the shoe.

In the treeing and packing department, the final finishing and dressing of the upper is done, and the shoes are inspected and packed. From here the boxed shoes are moved to the finished goods storage area to await shipment from the factory.

Table II-3 presents an approximate breakdown of costs for the production of medium-priced men's and women's shoes. It illustrates the high share of materials expenditure and the relative unimportance of machinery costs. Table II-4 gives a breakdown of labor and machine costs by departments for the production of men's Goodyear welted

TABLE II-3

Typical Cost Breakdown for Men's and Women's
Shoes, 1975

	Percent of total costs	
Item	Men's shoes, Goodyear process	Women's shoes cemented process
Materials	40	35
Direct labor	32	30
Supervision	10	15
Financing	9	9
Depreciation, rental of machinery, insurance, and maintenance	8	8
Other overhead	1	3
Total	100	100

SOURCE: Interviews.

shoes. The estimates demonstrate greater relative importance of labor
and machine costs in the making department.

The type of machinery used in the various processes is generally
not affected by the size of output. Higher levels of output are achieved
by installing a duplicate battery of equipment.

The greatest opportunity for realizing the potential economies of

TABLE II-4

Labor and Machine Costs by Main
Processes, 1975

Process	Direct labor costs as percent of total direct labor costs	Machine costs as percent of total machine costs
Cutting	20	25
Sewing	30	20
Making	45	50
Finishing	5	5
Total	100	100

SOURCE: Interviews.

specialization exist in the making department. In the other departments economies of scale are slight. Machinery utilization becomes more important in the making and cutting departments. Furthermore, since the output of operatives in the different departments varies, efficient utilization of equipment and manpower requires an adequate balancing of the output of the set of machines and workers. Otherwise, there will be excess capacity in some facilities when other facilities are running below capacity. Since the skill of operatives varies, the plant attempts to achieve balance by positioning the most competent operatives where skill levels are most crucial, by having one employee perform two tasks, and by assigning overtime to employees in some operations.

Clearly, the larger plants, apart from being able to better adjust and synchronize machines and operations, have an advantage because of their greater flexibility. There is more scope for maneuverability in the case of absenteeism, machine breakdown, or turnover of workers. On the other hand, the plants located at the lower end of the size distribution farm out certain operations or buy out soles and heels ready-made, or become subcontractors to larger companies. The cost penalty that a small plant would incur is thus limited. Another practice that operates in the same direction is the use of foremen as operatives in the smaller plants. Thus, any waste caused by the existence of spare time on their part is somewhat diminished. When we drop the assumption that input prices are not affected by scale, it becomes obvious that the advantages of a larger plant become more pronounced. For instance, a large firm obtains more favorable credit terms; this is crucial in an industry where material carrying costs are important.

Other Factors

It will be well to conclude this examination of the economies of scale with a few remarks on some other factors that affect the viability of a footwear manufacturing enterprise. The quality of management is the most decisive of these forces.[4] It engages in inspection and assortment of leather that is converted into footwear by over 200 operations

---

[4]M. Bryce, a senior economist of the industrial development consulting firm of Arthur D. Little, Inc., argues that this is equally true for other factors besides economies of scale: "No matter how good the financial structure or how outstanding the engineering, every project will ultimately succeed or fail on the strength of its management" [3, p. 158].

performed by skilled and unskilled workers. In addition, since footwear manufacturing is a cyclical industry, subject to seasonal fluctuations, a management that successfully maintains a steady flow of work may offset many disadvantages caused by operating at a suboptimal scale. A producer may realize a fairly even flow of work by owning retail outlets—as some companies do at present. In some instances, manufacturers may own a chain of retail shops or hold sufficient interest in them as to be able to exercise control over buying policy. Other ways of achieving an even flow of work is through subcontracting and putting out during the boom phase of the cycle. Design is particularly important for women's shoes and is becoming increasingly important for men's shoes. A flair for selecting successful styles and foreseeing trends in design is a significant factor affecting the viability of footwear firms.

One must also consider the variety of styles being fabricated in a plant, and here the concept of a production run is helpful. It is defined as the number of shoes of a particular style made before changing to another style. The length of the run is also determined by the type of leather used, the ability to forecast sales of each type and style, and the financing of stocks. The resultant economies caused by longer production runs express themselves in higher labor productivity and reduced costs of supervision. The increasing use of materials other than leather (such as vinyl, poromerics, and others) in the manufacturing of footwear [38, p. 11] will probably increase the relative importance of scale economies in this industry, since the uniform quality of the raw material would make it possible to lengthen the production run.

If a wide range of leather products is used and a variety of styles is fabricated, the difficulties encountered by a large plant may more than offset any economies obtained by specialization and a more effective balancing of machines and operations. On the other hand, a reduction in variety leads to difficulties in marketing. A large plant may overcome this dilemma by subcontracting those styles it does not wish to produce to a small plant. In this way, management is able to exploit the advantages of both specialization and marketing.

As to the problem of the quality of the finished product and its relationship to scale economies, industry sources assert that quality is primarily dependent on the time devoted to operations. Inasmuch as it is a function of time, it imposes lower productivity per worker and per machine in terms of number of pairs of shoes. Where such conditions prevail, the economies of scale operate over a lower range of output.

Two additional practices in the United States tend to limit the technical economies of scale. The first involves leasing of equipment whose rents are based predominantly on machine usage. In this case, an optimal plant cannot exploit all the potential advantages of lower machine costs. The second practice concerns compensation of workers by incentive plans. Since the production yield element in the plan, expressed in the payment of workers by piece rate, is the controlling one, it results in the efficient plants paying higher wages per worker, although not, of course, per pair of shoes made.

The account of economies of scale would not be complete without a comment concerning technological change. The optimum is a dynamic concept in that it changes as techniques change. The introduction of more technically advanced machinery and its wider acceptance and diffusion will probably raise the optimum size for plants specializing in them. However, the development of more automated equipment is hindered by the wide range of styles and sizes of shoes and the quality of leather. In addition, relatively small variations in the prices of the variable factors (about 80% of total cost) can easily offset any disadvantages caused by operating at less than the optimal scale. Equally important is the percentage of leather lost in the fabrication process. This depends on the skill of the operatives and the effectiveness of supervision. To summarize, an informed and competent management in controlling all these factors is undoubtedly more crucial to the profitability of a footwear enterprise than the economies of scale as traditionally measured.

In many other industries the prospect of success is based on the necessity for new firms to establish themselves on a very large scale. It is clear that the technical conditions of shoe manufacturing accord no such laurels of distinction to the large-scale plant as to greatly hamper a small plant in its attempts to survive. Requirements for working capital on the part of a small plant have been diminished through the plant's use of the subcontracting arrangements it develops either with supplying firms or wholesalers. Even where firms operate below minimum optimal size, the incomplete costing of management may confer a positive production advantage. Its viability is attributable to a multitude of socioeconomic forces. The preference for independence induces the owner to spend long hours of work at the plant and perform a variety of services that he does not value for costing purposes at anything approaching their market value. Surely, the mortality rate of the suboptimal plants is high, but some can still survive and compete successfully with the efficient firms.

Summary and Comparative Findings

The above discussion suggests that the main sources of scale economies for large plants stem from flexibility and the division, balancing, and synchronization of processes. The findings of plant economies are consistent and strongly suggest that the minimum optimal scale for medium-quality shoes is in the range of 250–499 persons employed; while for higher-quality shoes, or those requiring greater style variety, might even be in the range of 1–49 persons engaged. There is strong indications that the average cost curve is L-shaped, in the sense that economies of scale tail off as output increases.[5] It is also clear that the minimum optimal scale of a shoe plant is too small to obstruct entry, precludes the existence of a large number of plants within the industry, and prevents a high degree of competition. As a percentage of industry employment, minimum optimal scale of plant is of the order of 0.15–0.30 percent.

Our findings with reference to optimum plant size are not too much at variance with those arrived at by others in the United States and Europe. H. A. Silverman, in his cursory investigation of the British shoe industry in the early 1940s, concluded that efficient production was achieved by an industrial unit engaging 250–350 employees [10].

J. S. Bain, on the basis of questionnaire data sent to United States shoe manufacturers, roughly estimates the optimal plant scale to produce 2500–10,000 pairs of shoes per day [1, p. 230]. The study cites supplementary estimates of Bruce Cheek, based on field investigations, which tended to place optimal plant scale for men's dress shoes at 2400 pairs daily and for low-priced men's shoes at 6000 pairs daily [1, p. 230].

H. A. Simon and C. Bonini estimated, on the basis of the 1947 *Census of Manufactures's* statistics, the efficient output to be between 500 and 1200 pairs per day [70, pp. 606–617].

---

[5]Doubts have been expressed as to the very existence of diseconomies of scale "in the presence of modern administrative techniques." See Weiss [73, p. 247], and especially Ross [66]. Also see Wiles [11, chapter 12].

Finally, three further studies investigating the Irish [20, p. 29], British [9, p. 24], and Italian [7, p. 24] footwear industries concluded that optimal plant scale might produce 1200–4800 pairs daily and employ 120–250 workers.

In general, the estimated efficient range of output is much higher for the American than for the European footwear industries. The reason for this development lies in the fact that shoe manufacturing in the United States is characterized by longer production runs. Furthermore, quality differences in the product may exist, so we are really dealing with different production functions.

2.   TURNOVER OF FIRMS

Certain imperfections in the market have been found that, in combination, may pose a substantial deterrent to the prospective entrant. While technical scale economies are of no great significance (the minimum optimal plant size is very small relative to the market demand for footwear), entry barriers may arise from other sources.

The potential competitor at the manufacturing level is hampered by the existing distribution channels. Moreover, entry may be thwarted by the presence of product differentiation based upon brand name and working capital requirements.

On the other hand, entry is facilitated by the possibility of renting both floor space and equipment. A potential entrant has a reasonable chance of making a successful entry through highly specialized production and short runs or through the use of subcontracting arrangements that the plant develops either with larger firms or wholesalers. The venture can be initiated on a tiny scale for which small or moderate means are required, and then grow toward the upper end of the size distribution to a position of maturity.

A record of the number of failures in the industry reveals (Table II-5) a secular deceleration. Unfortunately, no data on plant closings as distinguished from company failures are available. Until 1963 the footwear industry's trade association reported annual figures on entry and exit. In the decade ending with 1963 its figures indicate that new firms entered the industry at the rate of 35–40 per year, while 45–47 firms left the industry each year. As noted in an earlier section, a substantial decline in both plants and employment in the industry has been under way throughout the whole post-World War II period. In other words,

TABLE II-5

Failures in the Footwear Industry and Trade
in Selected Years[a]

	Manufacturing		Wholesaling		Retailing	
Year	Number	Liabilities (thousand dollars)	Number	Liabilities (thousand dollars)	Number	Liabilities (thousand dollars)
1947	33	2196	5	204	14	169
1954	41	4248	8	403	97	1596
1958	41	9617	4	396	169	3855
1960	36	10,182	2	950	155	3974
1962	34	9473	5	407	160	4757
1964	22	5630	1	10	133	4545
1966	14	4798	6	1141	91	3329
1968	11	3253	2	170	53	1732
1970	14	5179	6	3091	69	3963
1972	7	1950	[b]	[b]	99	10,929
1973	8	16,410	[b]	[b]	125	6426

[a]This record includes businesses that ceased operations following assignment or bankruptcy; ceased with loss to creditors after such actions as execution, foreclosure, or attachment; voluntarily withdrew, leaving unpaid obligations; were involved in court actions such as receivership, reorganization, or arrangement; or voluntarily compromised with creditors.

[b]Not available.

SOURCE: Dun & Bradstreet and American Footwear Industry Association [75, p. 172].

the existing flow of new firms into the industry has not been sufficient to offset the increasing exit rate.

Such an easy entry and exit pattern of firms would imply that profit rates would not be allowed to remain either excessively high or low for long. This indeed seems to be the case, as demonstrated by the comparison of profit figures of selected footwear corporations with those of the clothing and apparel industry, which is known to be highly competitive in pricing and thus characterized by low profit rates (see Appendix Table II-A).

APPENDIX TO CHAPTER II

TABLE II-A

Comparison of Net Income of Leading Corporations
in the United States Footwear and Clothing
and Apparel Industries

| Year | Percent return on net worth | | Profit margins as a percent of gross sales | |
	Footwear	Clothing and apparel	Footwear	Clothing and apparel
1954	10.2	5.0	3.2	2.2
1955	11.4	6.9	3.5	3.1
1956	10.8	7.8	3.3	3.2
1957	10.8	6.7	3.4	2.9
1958	9.2	6.2	3.0	2.7
1959	11.2	10.5	3.3	3.6
1960	8.8	10.2	2.9	3.5
1961	5.4	10.7	1.8	3.5
1962	9.9	12.0	3.0	3.6
1963	8.1	12.0	2.6	3.4
1964	11.0	13.6	3.3	3.6
1965	12.3	16.3	3.5	4.3
1966	13.5	16.2	3.7	4.2
1967	13.1	13.6	3.6	3.7
1968	15.7	15.7	3.9	4.0
1969	12.5	13.4	3.3	3.6
1970	10.6	10.7	3.0	3.0
1971	10.8	10.8	3.0	3.1
1972	11.8	9.8	3.5	2.9
1973	8.4	9.1	3.1	2.6

SOURCE: The First National City Bank of New York, *Monthly Letter* (various issues).

THE WELFARE EFFECTS OF UNITED STATES TARIFF RESTRICTIONS ON IMPORTED FOOTWEAR

1. THEORY

A major target of our research effort will involve the measurement of the welfare effects that may be experienced as a result of trade liberalization in the footwear industry. These effects are expected to arise as the economy adjusts to trade liberalization by altering its domestic pattern of consumption and production to the shifting winds of international competition and, in the process, may reap more fully the benefits of specialization along lines of comparative advantage. It is well known that international trade confers two distinct advantages on a country: first, expanding its consumption opportunities—the consumption gain—and second, shifting resources into more productive areas—the production gain. In the process of international exchange, the real income of the country increases. In brief, it is clear that there is a real surplus to be gained through international exchange and that tariff restrictions tend to eat into that surplus. Therefore, the numerical estimate of that surplus, however imperfect, and its response to tariff policy should be an important parameter of commercial policy.

As a way of quantifying the welfare effects of trade restrictions, the needed theoretical framework will for the most part be based upon the extensive economic literature on the subject, drawing heavily upon the work done by John Floyd, Stephen Magee, Craig MacPhee, Giorgio Basevi, and others.[1]

While one of the most comprehensive theoretical treatments of the welfare implications of free trade versus restricted trade in a general equilibrium setting seems to be incorporated in Floyd's study, the work of Magee and MacPhee demonstrates how the partial equilibrium approach could be used profitably for the rough estimation of these welfare effects. Indeed, when the emphasis is on a single industry, the partial equilibrium setting, although less elegant, would be more applicable than the general equilibrium approach. We will first develop the former model in a static setting where no growth occurs in domestic demand. Later, the more realistic case of continually growing United States demand for footwear as a result of income and population changes will also be treated.

The partial approach may also help to fill a void in economic research in the sense that economists in general have preferred to analyze macroeconomic problems for which statistical data are abundant and readily available, to the almost total neglect of microeconomic problems. Harry Johnson expresses it succinctly as follows:

> Economic theorizing, research and policy discussions have tended to be excessively concerned with macroeconomic . . . to the neglect of microeconomic problems . . . whose solutions are likely over the long run to be more important to the achievement of a highly productive and rapidly growing economy.[2]

This study, with its particular orientation, is meant to remedy the situation, at least in part, by identifying, analyzing, and probing into the configuration of internal and external factors necessary for rational adjustment and to draw relevant lessons of experience therefrom.

The traditional analysis of the welfare effects of tariff restrictions is portrayed in Figure III-1 with the usual supply and demand curves and with imports entering at a price below the domestic equilibrium price that would prevail in the absence of trade. We assume that the

---

[1]See the References.
[2]See Johnson [57, pp. 68–79], quoted by Williamson [74, p. 112].

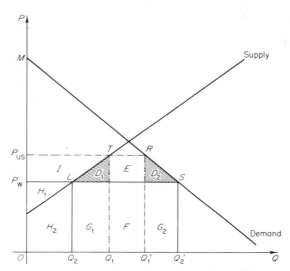

Figure III-1.   The welfare effects of a tariff.

world price of the importables is P_W, ruling out any terms of trade effects. In the absence of a tariff on United States imports of the product, the domestic demand for the product would equal OQ_2'. The quantity imported then is the difference between the domestic demand and supply Q_2Q_2'. The consumer surplus is the area MSP_W.

If we now impose a tariff on imports of the product, the price in the United States rises to OP_{US}; the *ad valorem* equivalent of the tariff is equal to $t = P_{US}P_W/OP_W$. Even though the tariff reduces the amount of consumer surplus by the area P_WSRP_{US}, part of the reduction in consumer welfare is captured by the domestic producers as rent (area I) and by the government as tariff revenue (area E). However, the area D_1 (the producer's dead-weight loss) and area D_2 (the consumer's dead-weight loss)[3] are captured by no one.

A thorny theoretical problem plagues welfare analysis: should the consumer surplus itself be taken from an ordinary demand curve or from a compensated demand curve? Whereas the ordinary demand curve indicates the quantity that a utility-maximizing consumer with a

[3]The classical Marshallian concepts of consumer's and producer's surplus have been clouded by controversy which appears to be still unresolved at this time. For a general survey, see Currie *et al.* [51] and Mishan [58]. Mishan's conclusion has been questioned by Shepherd [68].

given level of money income will demand at each price, the compensated demand curve indicates the quantity a consumer will demand at each price, assuming his money income is adjusted so that he remains on the original indifference curve. Unfortunately, no amount of observation would disclose the nature of the compensated demand curve in practice. It would require that a compensating variation in income be made which implies knowledge of the unknown utility structure. What is actually observed is the ordinary demand curve indicating purchases of importables as a function of money income and prices. The usual way out in relating the two demand curves is to assume a zero income elasticity of demand, which would then make them identical. This assumption is empirically reasonable, since the increase in income from a fall in footwear prices would be negligible. That is, the compensated demand curve indicates the substitution effect of a price change, while the ordinary demand curve reflects both the substitution and income effects of a price change. Graphically, a zero income effect implies parallel indifference curves at any quantity of the commodity. Accordingly, with the assumption of zero income effect, triangles under the ordinary demand curve will provide a measure of the consumer surplus.

Mathematically,

(1)
$$D_1 = \frac{1}{2} \Delta Q_s \Delta P$$

$$= \frac{1}{2} \left[Q_s E_s \left(\frac{\Delta P}{P} \right) \right] \frac{\Delta P}{P} P$$

$$= \frac{1}{2} E_s \left(\frac{\Delta P}{P} \right)^2 P Q_s$$

$$= \frac{1}{2} t^2 E_s V_s$$

where $E_s = (\Delta Q_s / \Delta P)(P/Q_s)$ and $\Delta Q_s = Q_s E_s (\Delta P/P)$, since $\Delta P/P = t$ and

Q_s = the quantity of domestic production
P = the domestic price of the product
E_s = the price elasticity of domestic supply
V_s = the dollar value of domestic production
t = the tariff rate

The same procedure will yield

(2)
$$D_2 = \frac{1}{2} \Delta Q_d \Delta P$$

$$= \frac{1}{2} \left[Q_d \eta_d \left(\frac{\Delta P}{P} \right) \right] \Delta P$$

$$= \frac{1}{2} \left[\eta_d \left(\frac{\Delta P}{P} \right)^2 Q_d P \right]$$

$$= \frac{1}{2} \left(\frac{\Delta P}{P} \right)^2 \eta_d V_d$$

$$= \frac{1}{2} t^2 \eta_d V_d$$

where $\eta_d = (\Delta Q_d / \Delta P)(P/Q_d)$ and $\Delta Q_d = \eta_d \Delta P (Q_d / P)$, and

η_d = the price elasticity of domestic demand
Q_d = the total quantity demanded domestically
V_d = the dollar value of total domestic consumption

Therefore, the total welfare costs of protection are

$$DWL = D_1 + D_2 = \frac{1}{2} (t^2 E_s V_s + t^2 \eta_d V_d)$$

In other words, the sum of D_1 and D_2 measures the total social costs to American consumers of United States tariff restrictions on the import good in question in that $D_1 + D_2$ represents the loss of surplus not captured by anyone.

To compute the social cost of the existing trade restrictions, we will need an estimate of the parameters E_s and η_d. The values of t, V_s, and V_d can be obtained from published statistics. However, bearing in mind that it is much easier to estimate the price elasticity of demand for the imported good (η_m), and since η_m, η_d, and E_s are all related to each other, we only have to estimate η_m and η_d empirically if E_s is difficult to estimate.

Starting with the equation

$$V_m = V_d - V_s$$

where

V_m = dollar volume of imports
V_d = dollar volume of domestic demand
V_s = dollar volume of domestic production

now

(3) $dV_m = dV_d - dV_s$

$$\eta_m = \left(dV_d - \frac{dV_s}{V_m}\right)\left(\frac{P}{dP}\right) \quad \text{since} \quad \eta_m = \frac{dV_m}{V_m}\left(\frac{P}{dP}\right)$$

$$= \left(\frac{dV_d}{V_m} - \frac{dV_s}{V_m}\right)\left(\frac{P}{dP}\right)$$

$$= dV_d\left(\frac{P}{dP}\right)\frac{1}{V_m} - dV_s\left(\frac{P}{dP}\right)\frac{1}{V_m}$$

$$= V_d\, dV_d\left(\frac{P}{dP}\right)\frac{1}{V_d V_m} - V_s\, dV_s\left(\frac{P}{dP}\right)\frac{1}{V_s V_m}$$

$$= \eta_d\left(\frac{V_d}{V_m}\right) - E_s\left(\frac{V_s}{V_m}\right) = \eta_d\left(\frac{V_d}{V_m}\right) - E_s\left(\frac{V_d - V_m}{V_m}\right)$$

$$= \eta_d\left(\frac{V_d}{V_m}\right) - E_s\left(\frac{V_d}{V_m}\right) + E_s\left(\frac{V_m}{V_m}\right)$$

$$= \frac{V_d}{V_m}\,(\eta_d - E_s) + E_s$$

For equation (3) we have to know only two out of the three price elasticities, since the third will then be determined automatically. The values of V_d and V_m can be obtained from published statistics.

Having derived the equations that will enable us to measure the welfare costs of the existing tariff restrictions on nonrubber footwear, it should be noted that the welfare costs estimated via these equations are annual flows—these losses are incurred every year. Therefore, we will have to estimate the present discounted value of eliminating the perpetual annual welfare costs. We will assume a static, no-growth case, in which the domestic demand for footwear is not growing, as a prelude to a more realistic analysis of the growth case later on.

The present value of this perpetual stream of welfare losses can be computed by using an appropriate social rate of discount i, such as the long-term bond rate. After having chosen i, the following equation will give us the present value of the costs:

$$PV_b = \frac{DWL_1}{(1 + i)} + \frac{DWL_2}{(1 + i)^2} + \frac{DWL_3}{(1 + i)^3} + \cdots + \frac{DWL_n}{(1 + i)^n}$$

where $n \to \infty$ and DWL is the welfare dead-weight loss. Since no growth is assumed,

$$DWL_1 = DWL_2 = DWL_3 = DWL_n$$

The above equation can then be reduced to

(4) $$PV_b = \frac{DWL}{i}$$

by using the geometric progression rule.

To calculate the welfare effects of eliminating the existing tariff restrictions, we must subtract the costs of moving resources out of the import-competing industry from the gains realized through the reduction in the inefficiencies (i.e., $D_1 + D_2$).

After obtaining the present discounted value of the latter costs, we can compute the net gain in welfare arising from trade liberalization:

$$PV_b - PV_c = \text{Net welfare gain}$$

where PV_c is the present discounted costs of moving resources out of the import-competing industry. We realize that there is no clean measure of the latter social cost, but we will try to compute a figure along the lines suggested by Magee.

The social cost of resource reallocation caused by trade liberalization is the value added lost by the released labor while searching for new jobs. For this, we will have to estimate the decrease in the output of the import-competing industry as a result of increasing imports, the marginal labor output coefficient l, and the length of duration of unemployment T.

First, the decrease in domestic production of the good in value terms can be shown as

$$\Delta V_s = V_s \left(\frac{\Delta P}{P} \right) + V_s \left(\frac{\Delta Q_s}{Q_s} \right) - \Delta Q_s \, \Delta P$$

Since

$$E_s = \left(\frac{\Delta Q_s}{Q_s} \right) \frac{P}{\Delta P}$$

$$\frac{\Delta Q_s}{Q_s} = E_s \left(\frac{\Delta P}{P} \right)$$

$$\Delta Q_s = Q_s E_s \left(\frac{\Delta P}{P} \right)$$

$$\Delta V_s = V_s\left(\frac{\Delta P}{P}\right) + V_sE_s\left(\frac{\Delta P}{P}\right) - PQ_sE_s\left(\frac{\Delta P}{P}\right)\left(\frac{\Delta P}{P}\right)$$

$$= V_s\left(\frac{\Delta P}{P}\right) + V_sE_s\left(\frac{\Delta P}{P}\right) - V_sE_s\left(\frac{\Delta P}{P}\right)^2$$

And since $t = \Delta P/P$,

(5) $\Delta V_s = V_st + V_sE_st - V_sE_st^2$

$$= tV_s(1 + E_s - tE_s)$$

Now that we have ΔV_s, which is the decrease in domestic production of the good brought about by trade liberalization, we can write an equation for the amount of labor to be released by ΔV_s:

(6) $\Delta L = l\,\Delta V_s$

where L is labor and $l = \Delta L/\Delta V_s$. To compute the value added lost by labor,

(7) $\Delta V_L = W\,\Delta LT$

where

V = value added lost by labor
W = the annual average wage
T = the duration of unemployment

Then, the present discounted value of the net welfare gain resulting from the elimination of the existing tariff on the product is, as stated earlier,

(8) $PV_b - PV_c$

In calculating the cost of resource reallocation, we have so far assumed that the displaced workers will be reemployed at the same wage rate as in the import-competing industry. However, if the type of labor employed in the shoe industry is a relatively scarce factor in the United States, it implies that the wages of displaced workers will be lower than their pretariff level. Both McCarthy [31] and Bale [12, p. 180] observed in their studies that when a displaced shoe worker is reemployed, the average hourly wage rate is somewhat lower than in the previous job. If the differential were of significant magnitude, we would have to add to the cost of resource reallocation the value of any reduction in wages that the reemployed workers have to absorb. Unless the worker makes up his wage differential in 1 year, we need to estimate the discounted value of his lifetime loss of wages due to this wage reduction from the present until the retirement age, so that

$$(9) \qquad PV_c = PV \text{ of } \Delta V_L + PV \text{ of the reduction in wages}$$

Turning to the more realistic case where the domestic demand for nonrubber footwear is growing over time at, say, $r\%$ per annum, the dead-weight loss estimate in year j can be written as

$$(10) \qquad DWL_j = \frac{1}{2} t^2 E_s V_s + \frac{1}{2} t^2 \eta_d V_d (1 + r)^j$$

It is assumed that there is no growth in the domestic production of the good. The present value of the DWL in year j can be written as

$$(11) \qquad PV_{bj} = \frac{(\frac{1}{2}) t^2 E_s V_s + (\frac{1}{2}) t^2 \eta_d V_d (1 + r)^j}{(1 + i)^j}$$

In order for the sum of the present values to converge, r must be less than i. Therefore, the present value of the dead-weight loss, including the growth in demand, is the sum of all future streams of dead-weight losses discounted at i, some social rate of capitalization. The net welfare gain through reductions in inefficiencies when there is growth in demand, becomes

$$(12) \qquad \sum_{j=1}^{\infty} PV_{bj} - \sum_{j=1}^{\infty} PV_c$$

The foregoing theoretical model is, of course, subject to a number of limitations which should be made explicit from the start:

1. The partial equilibrium approach assumes that removal of the tariff decreases the price of the good in question by the full amount of the tariff or, equivalently, that the terms of trade are not affected. It should be noted, however, that when a tariff is removed or lowered, the price of the good in the domestic market falls, thereby increasing consumption of that good. As imports increase, it may be necessary for foreign suppliers to increase their prices either because they cannot immediately tool up for production and/or because they have a less than perfectly elastic supply. Therefore, the removal or reduction of the tariff may not produce a price fall equal to the full amount of the tariff. That is, the country suffers a deterioration in terms of trade.

2. Regarding compensation to displaced factors, in traditional theory, the area above the supply curve and below the price line (area I

+ H_1 in Figure III-1) has been called the "producer's surplus." But, in addition, there will be adjustment losses to some resources that are not immediately absorbed into other industries. That is, the relevant part of area Q_2LTQ_1 in Figure III-1 must be added on to the loss in producer's surplus due to removal and/or tariff reduction. The argument then arises that transfer payments equivalent to the total loss incurred by displaced resources should be paid to them. Several problems immediately arise from this argument. For example, area $I + H_1$ in Figure III-1 is an indication of the excess payment that producers receive over that which would be necessary to make the same offer. If this is so, is it legitimate to conclude that producers should be compensated for losing what in effect is an economic rent? The nature of this rent is fundamentally quite different from that indicated by area Q_2LTQ_1, which represents a complete and immediate stoppage of all income to certain productive resources.

3. The analysis has been carried out as if domestic and imported shoes are perfect substitutes. If they are not, depending upon the degree of substitutability, there will persist some price differential between the two types of shoes, and the price elasticity of demand for each type of shoe will be less than it would otherwise be. Then the decrease in the prices of imported shoes caused by a tariff cut will have less of an impact on the domestic shoe industry. We feel that a priori the assumption of high substitutability between imported and domestic shoes seems reasonable in the basic model.

In our own work of evaluating the welfare effects of tariff restrictions on imported footwear, a variant of the above general model is developed so that perfect substitutability between imported and domestic footwear need not be assumed. The degree of substitutability is purposely left open for estimation via the cross price elasticities. These cross-elasticities turned out to be high, as our empirical work will show. In this section, therefore, we develop an analytical framework for the calculations of the annual costs of existing tariff restrictions on United States nonrubber footwear imports, in keeping with the foregoing refinements.

The initial empirical problem is to find the price elasticity for imported footwear as an aid in estimating the gain in consumer surplus associated with a given tariff reduction. As shown in Figure III-2, which depicts the United States demand curve for imported footwear, the price that prevails before the reduction in tariff is P_m and the

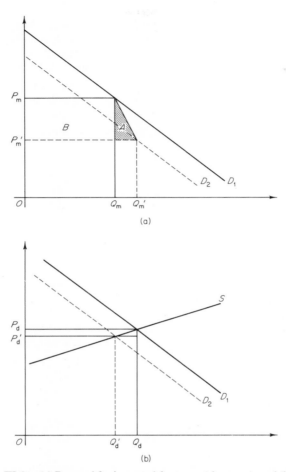

Figure III-2. (a) Demand for imported footwear (short run), and (b) demand and supply of domestic footwear.

corresponding quantity is Q_m. A decrease in the tariff by the amount OP_m/OP_m' (assuming negligible terms of trade effects) will decrease the domestic selling price of imported footwear from P_m to P_m', which results in an increase of imported shoes from Q_m to Q_m' in the short run. The increased purchase of imported footwear does not occur along the original import demand D_1 because as imported shoe price falls, consumers decrease their demand for domestic footwear. This, in turn, will certainly depress domestic shoe prices, since the short-run supply is less than perfectly elastic. In the face of softening domestic footwear prices, the import demand curve will shift to the left, as indicated by D_2. Of course, the magnitude of the leftward shift in the demand for domestic footwear will depend upon the degree of substitutability between the two goods. As explained earlier, this movement from restricted trade to freer trade results in an increase in consumer surplus equivalent to the area $A + B$. However, the net gain to society as a whole from this source alone is less than the total increase in consumer surplus, for the simple reason that part of the consumer surplus as indicated by area B represents a transfer of income from the government which loses tariff revenue by an equivalent amount. Therefore, the net gain is the triangular area under the line traced by the shift of the import demand curve. However, this is strictly a short-run phenomenon, for in a constant cost industry such as footwear, which is also highly competitive, the depressed prices will cause the marginal firms to incur losses. As their plants and equipment wear out, these firms will begin to leave the industry, thus decreasing the industry supply still further, as indicated by the shift of the supply curve from S_1 to S_2 in Figure III-3b. The contraction of the industry will stop when the price rises back to at least its former level, which will enable the existing firms to once again earn a normal return on their investment. In other words, the long-run supply of domestic footwear is most likely to be nearly perfectly elastic. This being the case, the import demand curve will revert to the original position indicated by D_1, as indicated in Figure III-3a, which makes the long-run increase in consumer surplus A' larger than the corresponding short-run consumer surplus indicated by A in Figure III-2a. Since most of the short-run adjustment will be completed in less than a year in the footwear industry, we will concentrate on the long-run analysis in our estimation of cost/benefit.

Once again, note that the analysis of consumer surplus holds strictly only if the demand curve is income-compensated rather than an ordinary demand curve that does not hold real income constant. Depending upon the importance of imported shoes in the total family budget and the income elasticity of demand for shoes, using the ordinary in place of the compensated demand curve would tend to overstate the price elasticity and the resultant gain in consumer surplus. However, even assuming that approximately 3% of the family budget is allocated for expenditure on shoes and an income elasticity as large as

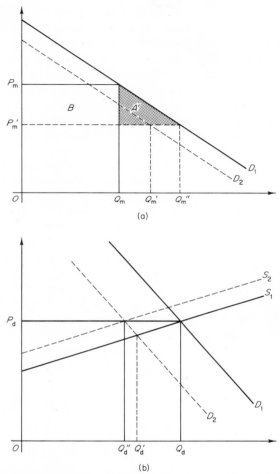

Figure III-3. (a) Demand for imported footwear (long run), and (b) demand and supply of domestic footwear.

5, would give a maximum error of 1.5% in overstating the consumer surplus for a 10% decline in shoe prices. Since the statistical estimation of the income-compensated demand is not possible, the ordinary demand curve must be used in the actual calculations of benefits from freer trade. Inasmuch as our empirical estimates detailed in the next section will show that imported and domestic footwear are very close

substitutes, we will take as an upper limit a decline of domestic footwear sales equivalent to the increase in purchases of imported footwear. This implies, quite plausibly, that consumers continue to purchase the same quantity of shoes at lower prices while substituting
more imported for domestic footwear.

In calculating the net gain to society as a result of a tariff reduction, the short-run relocation and adjustment costs associated with
the import-caused unemployment of labor and its reemployment
elsewhere, must be subtracted. Since the displacement costs of restricted trade are annual flows and recur every year, in estimating the
net gains from freer trade, we must calculate the present value using a
realistic social rate of discount such as the long-term bond rate.

So far, the consumer welfare loss not captured by either government or domestic producers that we have discussed is associated with
the existing tariff restrictions and is indicated by triangle a in Figure
III-4.

However, if we are to estimate the consumer dead-weight loss
stemming from a further increase in the tariff rate, say Δt, it must
include not only the additional triangle b but also the rectangle c. It is
obvious that the dead-weight loss resulting from the doubling of the
existing tariff rate to 20% would be approximately quadrupled. As can

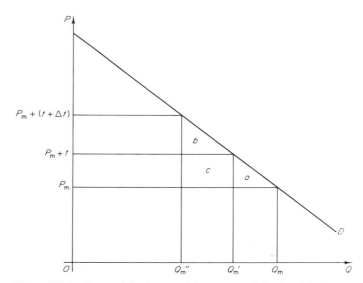

Figure III-4. Demand for imported footwear and dead-weight losses.

be seen from Figure III-4, the total area $a + b + c$ is four times as large as triangle a. Here, the case against further increases in the tariff on economic grounds alone becomes overwhelming.

If the trade restriction takes the form of an import quota—as advocated by the domestic industry—to achieve the same degree of protection as a given amount of tariff, the net social loss might be

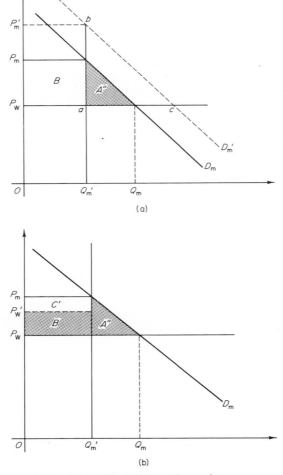

Figure III-5. The welfare effects of a quota.

larger. Assuming that import restriction is achieved by a quota, which raises the domestic price of imported footwear to the same level as P_m, as in the tariff case, Figure III-5 indicates that the loss in consumer surplus would be represented by the areas $A'' + B$. Unlike the tariff case, where part of the loss in consumer surplus B would be captured by the government as tariff revenue, the foreign suppliers might be able to raise their prices to P_w', thus capturing part of the consumer surplus lost, as indicated by area B' in Figure III-5b. This will certainly make the net welfare loss to society larger than in the tariff case. If foreign producers charge even the higher price of P_m, the net social loss would be correspondingly larger, as indicated by the areas $A'' + B' + C'$. The crucial question here is whether foreign suppliers of footwear can organize themselves as a cartel, a development unlikely to occur due to the large number of foreign footwear suppliers. If the foreign supply price remains constant in the face of the import quota, the licensed importers would capture part of the consumer surplus loss, as indicated by area B in Figure III-5a, or the government can capture all or part of B by imposing a varying amount of tariff or by auctioning off the import licenses. However, the case against quotas would become much stronger when we consider that, over time, demand for imported footwear will increase as shown by D_m' in Figure III-5a. This would cause the imported footwear price to rise, resulting in a much more rapid increase in consumer dead-weight loss than in the tariff case, as indicated by triangle abc in Figure III-5a.

2.   ESTIMATION OF PARAMETERS: METHODOLOGY AND DATA

The theoretical framework for estimating the parameters relevant to our study can be expressed by the following three structural equations:

$$Q_m = f\,(p_d, p_m, Y_r)$$
$$Q_d = g\,(p_d, p_m, Y_r)$$
$$Q_s = h(p_d, p_l, w, c_u)$$

where

Q_m = quantity imported of shoes
Q_d = Q_s = domestic production of shoes
p_d = domestic footwear price/general price index

p_m = imported footwear price/general price index
Y_r = real disposable income
p_l = price of leather/general price index
w = wage rate of footwear production workers/general price index
c_u = percent of capacity utilization

As the import demand equation indicates, we hypothesized that quantity of imports is determined by its own price, the price of domestic substitutes, income, and possibly a trend variable to capture the increase in imports due to unquantifiable factors such as aggressive marketing strategy and other promotional activities.

The demand for domestically produced footwear is assumed to be dependent upon its own price, the price of imports, and income.

As to the supply of domestically manufactured shoes, we hypothesized that the important explanatory variables are the price that shoe producers can get for their products and factors that usually affect supply, such as resource costs. We experimented with the price of leather, wage rate, expenditure on new machinery and equipment, and the capacity utilization rate. The latter has been attempted to determine whether bottlenecks existed in production and delivery as contended by industry sources. The above structural model will be the basis of our empirical work subject to appropriate modifications in defining the actual variables used.

Some of the variables are expressed on a per capita basis. This is justified partly because the underlying theory of consumer choice refers primarily to individuals and partly because per capita relationships are likely to be more meaningful and stable over time than relations between aggregates. Still, it may be argued that the use of per capita figures is not quite proper, since it gives all persons equal weight, regardless of age and sex, especially when a volatile item such as shoes is involved—women tend to purchase more pairs on the average than men; young adults spend more on shoes than elderly persons; etc. On balance, however, equal weights do not produce too much distortion, since the age and sex distribution of the population is fairly stable over time.

Regarding the time dimension to use in the estimating procedure, it should be kept in mind that consumer adjustment to price changes takes time and that as a result, the shorter the time period, the less elastic the demand will be. For example, a small price change may be an insufficient inducement at first to make a significant change in consumption. Over the longer period, however, as the differential persists, the advantage of changing from the more expensive domestic commodity to the cheaper imported one becomes more compelling. In the specific case of the demand for nonrubber footwear, such time lags may be unimportant if annual data are used. The effects of lags will be more important, the shorter the time period units utilized. For example, in quarterly data, current imports may be influenced more by prices in preceding quarters than by current prices. This is because of such factors as the lag between orders and shipments and the speed with which imports are adjusted to changes in prices.

In estimating the relevant parameters, we have tried the ordinary least-squares (OLS) method for the import demand equation and two-stage least-squares (TSLS) method for the domestic supply and demand equations. Moreover, since the price of domestically produced shoes (p_d) may not be completely exogenous in the import equation, we have also tried the TSLS method here. Even though there is no doubt that domestic shoe price should be treated as an endogenous variable in the domestic supply and demand equations, treating it as an exogenous variable in the import equation might not introduce too much bias if the world supply of footwear is highly elastic in the long run.[4]

In using the TSLS method, we have used all the exogenous variables in the system as instrumental variables for p_d, which is the only endogenous variable among the explanatory variables since its original values would produce biased estimates when correlated with the disturbance terms in each structural equation. In other words, the fitted values of p_d, $\hat{p}_d$, are substituted for the original values of p_d in estimating structural equations, thus involving two stages in the estimation procedure. Strictly speaking, the use of fitted values of p_d would still produce biased estimates for TSLS estimates, since consistent estimates are unbiased only when the sample size reaches infinity. However, if $E(p_d)$ instead of $\hat{p}_d$ could be used, the estimates would be unbiased, but the expected value of p_d is not known.

Most of the data used for estimation was obtained from official published statistics. However, we have encountered a great deal of difficulty in choosing appropriate price variables for imported footwear. No genuine import price indexes are available except either

---

[4]According to industry opinion, it is reasonable to assume that the long-run adjustment in the footwear industry is completed in less than 1 year.

unit-value indexes or value of imports and quantities from which unit-value indexes can be developed. As a result, two different versions of imported shoe prices were used, namely, a simple unit-value index for each category and a weighted average of unit-value indexes of sub-categories. In building our own price index for each category, we have bifurcated the sample period into two subperiods, 1964–1967 and 1968–1973.

In the first subperiod, 1964–1967, the frequent annual changes in Tariff Schedule of the United States Annotated (TSUSA) classifications necessitated the use of separate value weights in each year, whereas in the second subperiod, 1968 was used as a base year since the TSUSA items remain uniform thereafter. Data for the years prior to 1964 contained vastly different subcategories which precluded their use in constructing the weighted price index. In the case of the simple unit-value index, it was possible to extend the sample period back to 1955 when imports were still negligible.

In addition, Italian footwear prices were used as a proxy for imported footwear prices. Ideally, a better procedure would have been to use a weighted average of wholesale prices of all shoe exporting countries, but data constraints precluded us from doing this. It is worthwhile to note that Italian imports, the largest supplier to the United States market, have accounted for about 40% of total American footwear imports during the sample period. Footwear prices for Italy, denoted as p_{m4}, were developed in the following manner: We first obtained average wholesale prices per pair in principal Italian markets from *Annuario Statistico Italiano* for the years 1961–1973. Data for more recent years were not available. We then converted these average prices to a wholesale price index (WPI) with 1967 as the base year for groups of footwear and for total, using 1967 value weights derived from total United States footwear imports. Finally, the real Italian import price index was obtained by deflating the nominal Italian price index by the general United States wholesale price index for the years in question.

Since nonrubber footwear is not a homogeneous commodity but comprises a number of noncompeting categories based on sex, age, function, we subdivided the industry into as many as seven groups. These are men/boys footwear; women/misses; children/infants; work shoes; athletic shoes; slippers; and others. The latter consist mostly of vinyl footwear not classified by sex. We have also experimented with slightly different groupings such as adding male athletic and work shoes to the group of men/boys and female athletic shoes to the women/misses group. We have also tried aggregating slippers and others.

In the men/boys (M/B) category, we have tried first the simple unit-value index, denoted as p_{m_1}, obtained simply by dividing total dollar value of imports by the quantity of imports. In addition, we developed a more refined weighted unit-value index, denoted as p_{m_2}, which was obtained by weighting and adding some twenty-two TSUSA items.[5] As for the category of women/misses (W/M), the TSUSA items that entered into the construction of the refined weighted unit-value index numbered between ten and twenty-three, depending on the sub-period involved. There were fewer TSUSA items to deal with in the children/infants (C/I) group and in all other groups.

Theoretically, the refined weighted unit-value index should be superior to the simple unit-value index, especially if the relative importance of different TSUSA items changes substantially over time. However, note that the price index of the individual TSUSA items itself is still a unit-value index, and to the extent that TSUSA classifications changed from one subperiod to the next, it is not at all certain whether errors are reduced or compounded by the weighting procedure. The problem of compounding errors introduced by the weighted unit-value index, for example, would become more serious as the number of TSUSA items to be weighted increases, as in the case of (W/M).

As far as the domestic prices are concerned, the wholesale price index of shoes and its components were used, since WPI does not include imported shoes except for a negligible amount in the (W/M) group in later years. The consumer price index (CPI) of footwear and its components, by including imported shoe prices, was clearly not suitable for our purposes.

Empirical Findings

a   Total United States Footwear Market

In estimating the total United States demand for footwear including imports (sometimes denoted as composite demand) as well as the

[5]Details of construction for this index are shown in Appendix Table III-A. Note that the TSUSA items used are seven digits, the lowest level of disaggregation available in the official statistics.

supply and demand equations of domestically produced footwear, the appropriate quantity variable for a heterogeneous group of shoes seems to be the total money value of footwear deflated by its weighted price index. Clearly, the sum of the pairs of different categories of shoes would not be appropriate as the relevant quantity variable, as might be the case within each different category of footwear.

We have tried levels, logs, and log first differences, but the best equations in terms of high R^2, correct signs, and statistical significance of the coefficients of individual variables at the conventional levels, seem to be those expressed in logarithmic terms. At the same time, using log values has the added advantage of producing elasticity coefficient estimates directly.

First, the total demand for footwear has been estimated for the United States as

(1a) $\log \tilde{q}_c = 5.0213 - 0.4739 \log p_c + 0.2773 \log y$
$$(0.1679) \qquad (0.3528)$$
$$(-2.8218)^* \qquad (0.7860)$$

$$R^2 = 0.5444, \qquad F(2,7) = 4.1821, \qquad DW = 1.9258$$

where

$$
\begin{aligned}
R^2 &= \text{the coefficient of determination} \\
F &= \text{the } F \text{ statistic} \\
DW &= \text{the Durbin–Watson statistic}
\end{aligned}
$$

and where the dependent variable $\tilde{q}_c$ is per capita expenditure on footwear in constant dollars, p_c is the composite price index of domestic and imported footwear deflated by general CPI, and y is the real disposable per capita income. The equation number refers to Appendix Table III-A. The first set of figures in parentheses below the regression coefficients are the corresponding standard errors; the second set of figures in parentheses are the t values; * indicates significant t values at the 5% level; and when m appears, it indicates marginal significance. This arrangement holds uniformly throughout the text. A Glossary of Terms and the Data Sheet utilized in the Regression Analysis are to be found at the end of the text.

As can be seen, the price elasticity of demand for footwear in general is quite low, as indicated by the elasticity coefficient of −0.47. The income elasticity is also very low and not statistically different from zero. Such low price elasticity should be reasonably expected for necessities like shoes. Houthakker and Taylor, for example, in their estimated United States demand for footwear between 1929 and 1970, found a price elasticity coefficient of -0.09, which turned out to be not statistically significant. The explanation given for this phenomenon is of interest and is quoted here:

> Prices are less important in explaining U.S. consumption (of shoes) . . . The lack of a strong overall influence of prices is consistent with the predominance of habit formation . . . Prices should be expected to exert less of an influence on consumption at high levels of income because income becomes less of a constraining factor and because more commodities become subject to habit formation [5, pp. 153–154].

Since total footwear consumption, including imports in the United States has increased in real terms at the annual average rate of less than 1% between 1963 and 1973, while footwear prices have not declined relative to other prices, the population growth of about 1% per year seems to account for the increase in footwear demand entirely. The percentage changes in the value of footwear consumption were computed on the basis of information presented in the Data Sheet.[6]

Next, in estimating the total demand for imported footwear, the appropriate dependent variable should be the total value of imported footwear deflated by the general weighted price index of imported shoes. However, due to unavailability of appropriate data for the enlarged sample period, the simple unit-value index (p_{m_1}) must be used, yielding the total number of pairs of diverse categories. The total demand for imported footwear that has been estimated with per capita consumption of imported shoes as the dependent variable is

(2a)

$$\log \tilde{q}_m = -53.7314 + 4.1223 \log p_d - 1.3045 \log p_{m_1} + 5.2199 \log y$$
$$(1.2666) \qquad (0.1403) \qquad (0.3684)$$
$$(3.2546)^* \qquad (-9.2980)^* \qquad (14.1698)^*$$

$$R^2 = 0.9918, \qquad F(3.14) = 565.68, \qquad DW = 0.9908$$

The import price elasticity is -1.3 and statistically very significant, and the cross-elasticity is about 4, also statistically significant. Note that while the magnitude of the import price elasticity differs between our

[6]In 1955 the value of total footwear consumption, including imports, stood at $1.98 billion and in 1973 at $4 billion, which is an increase of 100%. Footwear prices increased by 80% during the same period, which would make the increase in real consumption of footwear 20% during the 19 year period. This makes the annual rate of increase less than 1% per annum.

study and that of Wayne Simon for the International Trade Commission (ITC), imports in both studies are several times more responsive to domestic price changes, as shown by much larger cross-elasticities than in their own price. This phenomenon may perhaps be due to the fact that domestic prices are generally higher in absolute terms—twice as high on the average. Likewise, Zabrowski (of the United States Department of Commerce), in his "price gap hypothesis," suggests that the large gap between domestic and imported shoe prices means that rises in the former induce more people with marginal demand to shift to cheaper imported substitutes, whereas rises in the latter do not compensate sufficiently for the already existing large price gap and hence, do not encourage many people to switch to the still more expensive domestic footwear.[7]

The income variable, with its relatively large elasticity coefficient, seems to have captured the effect of other variables that have contributed to the upsurge in imports. These other factors, which might not be quantifiable but are just as important, could be the development of new and more effective market strategies by importers—the offering of greater variety in style and workmanship in the import mix, not generally available from domestic sources at equivalent prices.

Using the ratio of imported and domestic footwear prices, p_{m_1}/p_d, does not seem to change the magnitude of the coefficients appreciably, as shown by equations (3a) and (4a), which is the same as (3a) but corrected for autocorrelation:

$$(3a) \quad \log \tilde{q}_m = -44.7154 - 1.4017 \log \frac{p_{m_1}}{p_d} + 6.6081 \log y$$

$$\phantom{(3a) \quad \log \tilde{q}_m = } (0.2391) \qquad\qquad (0.4102)$$
$$\phantom{(3a) \quad \log \tilde{q}_m = } (-5.8626)^* \qquad\quad (16.1089)^*$$

$$R^2 = 0.9659, \qquad F(2,16) = 226.81, \qquad DW = 0.5505$$

Using the ratio of prices has the advantage of preventing any intercorrelation that might have existed between the two price variables from biasing the elasticity estimates.

The addition of a trend variable t to the above specifications seems to raise the import price elasticity to -1.58 and -1.74, although the trend variable itself turned out insignificant, as reported in equations (5a) and (6a) of Appendix Table III-A.

[7]This point was raised by Jay D. Rubenstein of the University of Michigan.

Recognizing the deficiency of our dependent variable, we have also experimented with nominal dollar values for the dependent variable v_m on a per capita basis, while adding general WPI as an extra independent variable to account for price changes in other variables. Equation (7a) in Table III-A indicates that the import price elasticity and the income elasticity are not too much at variance with the above findings. Instead of deflating the dependent variable by population, we also entered the population as an independent variable, with disappointing results.[8]

The foregoing results show that most of our estimates of import price elasticity fall between -1.3 and -1.8. Choosing -1.5 as the most reasonable estimate of import price elasticity implies that if imported shoe price were to fall by 10% for whatever reason, imports of shoes would increase by 15%. The fact that our estimate of cross-elasticity of demand for imports with respect to domestic shoe price is between 4 and 7 suggests a very high degree of substitutability between imported and domestic shoes. This implies that a 1% rise in the price of domestic shoes would tend to increase imports of shoes by 4–7%.

Finally, we attempted to estimate import demand as well as the demand and supply of domestically produced footwear by the TSLS method using as instrumental variables for p_d all the predetermined variables that appeared in the structural model,

$$q_m' = \alpha_0 + \alpha_1 p_d' + \alpha_2 p_m' + \alpha_3 y'$$
$$q_d' = \beta_0 + \beta_1 p_d' + \beta_2 p_m' + \beta_3 y'$$
$$Q_s' = \lambda_0 + \lambda_1 p_d' + \lambda_2 p_\ell' + \lambda_3 w'$$

where $'$ indicates the log values of the variables.

No usable results have been obtained with regard to the demand for either imported or domestic footwear, while the supply of domestic footwear seems to have been easily identified via the TSLS method. The apparent difficulty in identifying and estimating the demand for domestic footwear seems to be due to its constant shifting. This is caused mainly by imports which, on the other hand, facilitated the identification and estimation of the domestic supply function as indicated by

[8]Another specification, quantity imported, was used as the independent variable and the price of imports was used as the dependent variable. The results are shown in equation (8a) of Table III-A; they seem to suggest a larger import price elasticity of -2, but the estimate is marred by its statistical insignificance and also by the wrong sign of some of the other independent variables.

(9a)

$$\log \tilde{Q}_s = -4.4424 + 4.5645 \log \hat{p}_d - 0.7329 \log p_\ell - 2.4697 \log w$$
$$\quad\quad\quad\quad\quad (1.2793) \quad\quad\quad\quad (0.6013) \quad\quad\quad\quad (0.6946)$$
$$\quad\quad\quad\quad\quad (3.5678)^* \quad\quad (-1.2187) \quad\quad\quad (-3.5554)^*$$

$$R^2 = 0.6908, \quad F(3,14) = 10.43, \quad DW = 1.7171$$

When a new specification for the supply was tried with price as the dependent variable and capacity utilization, c_u, as one of the explanatory variables, the following equation was obtained:

(10a)

$$\log p_d = 1.7846 + 0.1089 \log p_\ell + 0.4447 \log w + 0.4564 \log c_u$$
$$\quad\quad\quad\quad (0.0698) \quad\quad\quad (0.0436) \quad\quad\quad (0.1323)$$
$$\quad\quad\quad\quad (1.5604) \quad\quad\quad (10.2044)^* \quad\quad (3.4496)^*$$

$$R^2 = 0.9280, \quad F(4,12) = 72.999, \quad DW = 1.2012$$

The coefficient of c_u turned out to be 0.456, implying that a 10% increase in capacity utilization rate raises marginal cost and thereby price by about 5.5% within a 1 year period. The assumption of a less than perfectly elastic short-run domestic supply curve, as in our earlier theoretical construct, seems to have been borne out by the statistical evidence. However, the coefficient of c_u might well be biased upward because of the endogeneity in the domestic demand and supply model. At any rate, the supply of domestic footwear turned out to be highly price elastic. The price of leather (p_ℓ) and the wage rate (w) of production workers in the industry also turned out to be statistically significant explanatory variables.

If we turn to the estimation of the relevant parameters in various noncompeting footwear groups, we see that the same analytical framework has been retained. The detailed analysis of the two major groups—men/boys and women/misses—as well as other groups, follows.

b Men/Boys Footwear (M/B)

In this major group, we have first estimated the total demand for M/B footwear (composite of domestic and imported shoes) as

(1b)

$$\log \tilde{q}_c = 2.6813 - 0.2183 \log p_c + 0.3819 \log y$$
$$\quad\quad\quad\quad (0.1442) \quad\quad\quad (0.3400)$$
$$\quad\quad\quad\quad (-1.5139)m \quad\quad (0.1124)$$

$$R^2 = 0.2489, \quad F(2,7) = 1.16, \quad DW = 1.4775$$

where the dependent variable is the total value of M/B footwear consumption deflated by the appropriate price index on a per capita basis for this group. The equation number refers to Appendix Table III-B. Both the price and income elasticities are very close to zero, conforming to the results obtained in the estimation of total footwear consumption for the United States. This implies that population growth is the single most important determinant of demand for footwear.

Turning to the estimation of the import demand function for M/B footwear, the following equation was obtained using the per capita consumption of imported footwear as the dependent variable and the simple unit-value index for the import price variable:

(2b)
$$\log q_m = -41.3407 + 1.9678 \log p_d - 0.3469 \log p_{m_1} + 4.3456 \log y$$
$$\quad\quad\quad\quad\quad (2.3584) \quad\quad\quad (0.2043) \quad\quad\quad (0.9691)$$
$$\quad\quad\quad\quad\quad (0.8344) \quad\quad (-1.6979)m \quad\quad (4.4838)*$$

$$R^2 = 0.9741, \quad\quad F(3,10) = 125.6, \quad\quad DW = 1.0722$$

In other words, the dependent variable was obtained by deflating quantity imported of M/B footwear by subpopulation of M/B, which was determined (through industry consultation) to be male, ages 10 and above. Admittedly, this way of estimating subpopulation size relevant to footwear is somewhat arbitrary in the sense that there is no precise correspondence between shoe size and age of wearer.[9]

A slightly different specification of equation (2b) was also tried, by using the ratio of the two prices as an independent variable rather than entering them separately. Consistent results were obtained, as shown in equation (3b) of Appendix Table III-B. These equations have an extremely good fit, as indicated by the high R^2 and F ratios. However, it is somewhat surprising to see such a high income elasticity, whereas the own price elasticity seems somewhat on the low side.

In an effort to estimate the "true" income elasticity of demand, a trend variable t was inserted along with income, as shown in equations (4b) and (5b) (in Appendix Table III-B):

[9] The terms "men," "youth," and "boys" are used as in the TSUSA to differentiate size categories of footwear for males as follows: "men" refers to footwear of American men's size 6 and larger and "youths" and "boys" to American youths' size 11½ and larger but not as large as American men's size 6. The term M/B will be used in general to refer to footwear intended for youths and boys as well as for men. (See various Tariff Commission reports.)

(4b)

$$\log q_m = -34.0770 - 0.6407 \log p_{m_1}/p_d + 4.7312 \log y + 0.0881 \log t$$

$$
\begin{array}{ccc}
(0.4766) & (0.4769) & (0.1213) \\
(-1.3444)m & (9.9188)^* & (0.7259)
\end{array}
$$

$$R^2 = 0.9741, \quad F(3,10) = 125.58, \quad DW = 1.1637$$

Apparently, the inclusion of the trend variable did not materially reduce the income coefficient, and trend itself turned out to be insignificant. It is interesting to note that replacing the simple unit-value index (p_{m_1}) with the weighted unit-value index (p_{m_2}) produced similar results, as indicated by equations (6b) and (7b) in Table III-B. However, the poor performance of the price variables might be attributed to the errors inherent in the aggregation procedure used in the construction of the weighted unit-value index.[10]

For some of the reported import demand equations that showed a relatively low DW statistic, we have obtained new regressions by applying the Cochrane–Orcutt iterative technique, thus reducing the positive autocorrelation in the residuals. As shown by equations (10b)–(12b) in Table III-B, in general, the size of the coefficients of price variables p_d and p_m and their t values increased markedly. However, it is not certain how these results should be evaluated, since the DW ratios, even if low, are still in the inconclusive region.

Finally, the import demand was estimated by the TSLS method with more or less uniform results, as shown by equation (13b) in Table III-B.

Our attempts to estimate the structural equation—again using the TSLS method—representing the demand for domestic M/B footwear has met with little success, presumably because of the difficulty in correctly identifying the demand function, which seems to have shifted much more frequently than the corresponding supply function.

Looking at the reported demand function (14b), we see that the price elasticity of demand is marginally significant, whereas the income and the cross-elasticity of demand with respect to the import price coefficients are not significantly different from zero. Apparently, the

---

[10]Additionally, another version of the per capita consumption of imports was attempted by adding athletic and work shoes to the M/B group, with similar results, as indicated by equations (8b) and (9b) in Appendix Table III-B.

nonzero restriction of the coefficients in the specification of the above provides no assurance of their being so statistically:

(14b)
$$\log q_d = 8.0368 - 1.7111 \log \hat{p}_d - 0.1112 \log p_{m_2} + 0.0846 \log y$$

$$\begin{array}{cccc} & (1.6977) & (0.4835) & (0.8478) \\ & (-1.0078)m & (-0.2301) & (0.0997) \end{array}$$

$$R^2 = 0.6411, \quad F(3,6) = 3.57, \quad DW = 1.548$$

However, the estimation of the domestic supply equation along the same lines has been more successful, as shown by

(15b)
$$\log \tilde{Q}_s = -13.9056 + 6.4528 \log \hat{p}_d - 0.2552 \log p_\ell - 3.0384 \log w$$

$$\begin{array}{cccc} & (2.2757) & (0.2888) & (1.3247) \\ & (2.8355)^* & (-0.8833) & (-2.2937)^* \end{array}$$

$$R^2 = 0.6755, \quad F(3,10) = 12.67, \quad DW = 1.6058$$

where the dependent variable is the value of domestic production deflated by the relevant price index. The price coefficient of 6.45 indicates a highly elastic supply response of producers to footwear price changes, while the leather price and wage rate coefficients have the expected signs.

    In summary, even though the import price elasticity of demand for the M/B group is greater than that of the total demand for M/B (composite of domestic + imports) as is usually expected, it is somewhere around -0.5. The cross-elasticity of demand for imported footwear with respect to prices of domestic footwear is about 2, while the income elasticity is approximately 4. The simple unit-value index (p_{m_1}) fared better than the supposedly superior-weighted unit-value index (p_{m_2}), possibly because of compounding errors of aggregation and related problems, as mentioned earlier. Our attempts to estimate the demand for domestic footwear have not been too productive because of the difficulty in identifying it statistically. Supply for domestic footwear has been easier to identify and estimate, presumably because demand fluctuated much more than supply over the sample period. The price elasticity of supply is about 6, whereas the price elasticity of demand for domestic footwear is about -1.7, bearing in mind that it is only marginally significant.

(c) Women/Misses Footwear (W/M)

With regard to this other major group, the same type of regressions were conducted. The total demand for the W/M/C/I group (composite of domestic and imported footwear) is indicated by

(1c) $\log \bar{q}_c = 5.0214 + 0.2773 \log p_c - 0.4739 \log y$

$$\begin{array}{cc} (0.3528) & (0.1679) \\ (0.7859) & (-2.8218)^* \end{array}$$

$$R^2 = 0.5444, \qquad F(2,7) = 4.8, \qquad DW = 1.9258$$

(The equation number refers to Appendix Table III-C.) Again, both the price and income elasticity turned out very low and in line with the results previously obtained with regard to the total and M/B composite demand. Note that we were not able to estimate separate composite demand functions for W/M and C/I due to data constraints. However, no great damage is done, since C/I footwear represents a small component in relation to W/M footwear. On the other hand, in the estimation of import demand as well as domestic supply and demand functions, we were able to separate the two groups.

In estimating the import demand function for W/M, we first used the simple unit-value index (p_{m_1}) with the following result:

(2c)

$$\log q_m = -64.9431 - 1.9648 \log p_{m_1} + 6.4056 \log p_d + 8.2658 \log y$$

$$\begin{array}{ccc} (0.1621) & (1.2554) & (0.4607) \\ (12.1200)^* & (5.1026)^* & (17.9411)^* \end{array}$$

$$R^2 = 0.9814, \qquad F(3,10) = 229.3, \qquad DW = 1.6678$$

This equation as well as equation (3c) in Appendix Table III-C, whose price variable is in ratio form, indicate the import price elasticity of approximately -2 for the W/M footwear group. This is much larger than that for M/B. Both the cross-elasticity and income elasticity are very high. A possible reason why the price elasticity of demand for W/M is higher than that of M/B may be the fact that the per capita consumption of shoes for this group is higher than for M/B (i.e., in 1973 it was 4.23 pairs for W/M as against 1.94 pairs for M/B; per capita consumption of imported footwear was 2.05 and 0.63 pairs for W/M and M/B, respectively), and because shoes have not only strict utility but also ornamental and decorative value for W/M. The latter phenomenon is associated to a large extent with the more frivolous, attractive shoes, which the industry offers at a price that permits several shoes to fit into a place in the budget preempted by one or two pairs. Our findings are therefore consistent. Such a result would also be expected by economic theory, which suggests that luxury goods tend to be more price elastic than necessities.

The cross-elasticity estimate is also much higher in this group than for M/B. In both groups, the cross-elasticities are several times higher than own price elasticities, in keeping with the assymetrical response of consumers to these two price changes that were previously noted for the entire footwear market.

Adding a trend variable t, along with the same independent variables as before, did reduce the income elasticity somewhat, while the trend variable itself turned out to be statistically insignificant, as shown by equation (4c) in Appendix Table III-C. Attempts to estimate the import demand using the refined weighted unit-value index (p_{m_2}) for this group have not been successful, as reported in equations (5c) and (6c) in Table III-C. The import price elasticity in every case had the wrong sign, even though other explanatory variables continued to turn out to be plausible. Again, the poor performance of the weighted unit-value index can be attributed to biases introduced by the aggregation procedure. This problem appears to be most serious in the W/M group, for it is in said group that we find the largest number of TSUSA items to be aggregated. We have examined the components of this index with no definite conclusion regarding the nature and direction of this bias. Another source of error could be due to the impossibility of using a precise subpopulation group in deriving the per capita consumption of imported shoes. Subpopulation was defined to be female, over 10 years of age, since it is generally believed that the size of W/M shoes begins with size 4, roughly corresponding to girls aged 10. [11]

Applying the TSLS method to estimate the import demand for this group was not very productive. However, the results we have obtained for demand and supply functions of domestic footwear using the same method were much more encouraging. In fact, the supply function of domestic footwear seems to have been easily identified,

[11]The terms "women" and "misses" are used as in the TSUSA to differentiate size categories of footwear, not age of wearer, as follows: "women" refers to footwear of American women sizes 4 and larger and "misses" refers to American misses sizes 12½· and larger but not as large as American women's size 4. (See various Tariff Commission reports.)

while the estimation of the demand function is less tractable. The demand and supply equations, where the instrumental variables used for p_d were y, p_{m_1}, p_ℓ, and w, are

(7c)

$$\log q_d = 22.6328 - 1.9920 \log \hat{p}_d + 5.1501 \log p_{m_1} - 1.8784 \log y$$
$$\quad\quad\quad\quad\quad (1.9091) \quad\quad\quad (0.8038) \quad\quad\quad (0.7373)$$
$$\quad\quad\quad\quad (-1.0435) \quad\quad\quad (0.6408) \quad\quad\quad (-2.5473)*$$
$$R^2 = 0.8192, \quad F(3,6) = 8.133, \quad DW = 1.638$$

(8c)

$$\log Q_s = -14.3177 + 5.2303 \log \hat{p}_c - 0.3061 \log p_\ell - 3.7846 \log w$$
$$\quad\quad\quad\quad\quad (1.7775) \quad\quad\quad (0.4611) \quad\quad\quad (0.9459)$$
$$\quad\quad\quad\quad (2.9425)* \quad\quad (-0.6638) \quad\quad\quad (-4.0012)*$$
$$R^2 = 0.8192, \quad F(3,6) = 8.925, \quad DW = 1.8247$$

Note that while the demand is expressed in terms of per capita consumption of shoes, the supply is expressed in total quantity, as it should be. The price elasticity of demand for domestic footwear seems reasonable in magnitude even though it is marginally significant. The negative income term must capture the recent trend for continually declining sales of domestic footwear (attributable to not easily quantifiable factors such as better market strategies adopted by importers and increasing variety and styles of imported footwear).

Looking at both the demand and supply equations, it seems obvious that larger shifts in demand relative to supply have identified much more readily the supply equation. The price elasticity of supply is about 5, which is highly plausible and statistically significant, along with the wage rate coefficient w; the price of leather (p_ℓ), however, turned out to be statistically insignificant. Using a slightly different set of instrumental variables for p_d produced similar results for both demand and supply, as shown by equation (9c) in Appendix Table III-C.

To sum up, the price elasticity of imports for W/M footwear is approximately -2, which is higher than the average import price elasticity of about -1.5. This result should be expected in view of the fact that M/B (one of the two major groups) has a lower than average import price elasticity. The cross-elasticity of imports with respect to domestic footwear prices is about 6.4, while the income elasticity is about 8. The above estimates are based upon regression results using the simple unit-value index (p_{m_1}), since the weighted unit-value index (p_{m_2}) yielded no usable estimates of import price elasticity. The price elasticity of demand for domestic footwear seems to be around -1.7, while price elasticity of domestic supply is about 5.

(d) Children/Infants Footwear (C/I)

This minor group[12] has been investigated, and the results for the import demand function, using the weighted unit-value index (p_{m_2}) and per capita consumption, produced the following results:

(1d)
$$\log q_m = -62.9736 + 3.4745 \log p_d - 1.0742 \log p_{m_2} + 6.4541 \log y$$
$$\qquad\qquad\quad (1.6898) \qquad\quad (0.8184) \qquad\quad\quad (0.8297)$$
$$\qquad\qquad\quad (2.0561)^* \qquad (-1.3174) \qquad\quad (7.7785)^*$$

$$R^2 = 0.952, \qquad F(3,6) = 39.71, \qquad DW = 1.97$$

(The equation number refers to Appendix Table III-D.) The results imply that the import price elasticity is about unitary, which is higher than that for M/B but lower than that for the W/M group. The income elasticity and cross-elasticity continue to be high in this group.

An alternative specification using the ratio of prices was tried, with similar results, as reported in equation (2d) in Appendix Table III-D.

The TSLS method was also tried here, using as the instrumental variables for p_d all the exogenous variables in the system, namely p_m, p_ℓ, y, and w, with similar estimates of the coefficients as

(3d)
$$\log q_m = -63.3411 + 3.6624 \log \hat{p}_d - 1.1188 \log p_{m_2} + 6.4174 \log y$$
$$\qquad\qquad\quad (1.7575) \qquad\quad (0.8241) \qquad\quad\quad (0.8358)$$
$$\qquad\qquad\quad (2.0839)^* \qquad (-1.3577) \qquad\quad (7.6781)^*$$

$$R^2 = 0.952, \qquad F(3,6) = 39.62, \qquad DW = 1.94$$

Again applying TSLS, we have estimated the demand for domestic footwear as

(4d) $$\log q_d = 38.047 - 2.3060 \log \hat{p}_d - 4.0893 \log p_{m_2} - 1.0899 \log y$$
$$\qquad\qquad\quad (28.1437) \qquad\quad (13.2368) \qquad\qquad (13.4291)$$
$$\qquad\qquad\quad (-0.0819) \qquad (-0.3089) \qquad\quad (-0.0812)$$

$$R^2 = 0.062, \qquad F(3,6) = 0.132, \qquad DW = 2.81$$

[12]In 1973 the dollar value of imports for this group amounted to $25 million as opposed to $534 million for W/M and $277 million for M/B group.

As can be seen, none of the coefficients seem statistically significant even though the price elasticity of demand of 2.3 appears reasonable in magnitude. The identification of the demand for domestic footwear statistically seems to be quite difficult, as has been consistently true in the other groups.

On the other hand, the supply of domestic footwear was much more readily identifiable, obviously, because the demand schedule has shifted much more than the supply during the sample period. The supply equation is given by

(5d)
$$\log Q_s = -7.0328 + 3.8226 \log \hat{p}_d - 0.8057 \log w - 3.9063 \log p_\ell$$
$$ (0.9660) \qquad\quad (0.1781) \qquad\quad (0.7247)$$
$$ (3.9570)^* \qquad (-4.5239)^* \qquad (-5.3904)^*$$

$$R^2 = 0.951, \qquad F(3,6) = 27.79, \qquad DW = 3.0129$$

In summary, the price elasticity of import demand for C/I footwear is about unitary, while the income and cross-elasticity are 6.5 and 3.5, respectively. The estimation of domestic demand for this group has not been successful, whereas the price elasticity of supply has been estimated to be 3.8.

(e) Other Footwear Categories

Attempts to estimate the relevant structural parameters for other footwear groups comprising athletic, work shoes, and slippers have met with varying degrees of success.

As far as the slippers category is concerned, the import demand equation, with the per capita consumption of imported slippers as the dependent variable and the weighted unit-value index (p_{m2}) as one of the independent variables, has produced plausible results:

(1e) $\quad \log q_m(\text{Slp}) = -32.3027 - 0.9072 \log \dfrac{p_{m2}}{p_d} + 4.2660 \log y$

$$\phantom{(1e) \quad \log q_m(\text{Slp}) = -32.3027 } (0.2625) \qquad\qquad (0.9251)$$
$$\phantom{(1e) \quad \log q_m(\text{Slp}) = -32.3027 } (-3.4555)^* \qquad\quad (4.6113)^*$$

$$R^2 = 0.7543, \qquad F(2,7) = 10.74, \qquad DW = 1.8092$$

(The equation number refers to Appendix Table III-E.) The import price elasticity close to unity seems comparable to that of the C/I group.

The demand for domestic slippers, which was attempted using TSLS, has not been identified statistically, whereas the domestic supply of slippers seems to have been identified, as indicated by

(2e)
$$\log Q_s(\text{Slp}) = -1.3657 + 2.5887 \log \hat{p}_d - 0.7442 \log p_\ell$$
$$\qquad\qquad\qquad (1.1569) \qquad\quad (0.6247)$$
$$\qquad\qquad\qquad (2.2375)^* \qquad (-1.1912)^*$$

$$\qquad - 1.8469 \log w - 0.2548 k_n$$
$$\qquad\quad (1.2413) \qquad\quad (0.1036)$$
$$\qquad\quad (-1.4879) \qquad (2.4593)^*$$

$$R^2 = 0.6397, \qquad F(4,5) = 4.995, \qquad DW = 2.1285$$

Regarding work shoes, the import demand per capita, using the weighted unit-value index (p_{m_2}), again seems to have produced good results, as indicated by equations (3e) and (4e) (in Appendix Table III-E):

(3e)
$$\log q_m(\text{Wk}) = -5.4403 + 4.3299 \log p_d - 12.4294 \log p_{m_2} + 4.8845 \log y$$
$$\qquad\qquad\qquad (10.3219) \qquad\quad (5.0493) \qquad\qquad (5.4914)$$
$$\qquad\qquad\qquad (0.4195) \qquad\quad (2.4616)^* \qquad\qquad (0.8895)$$

$$R^2 = 0.8602, \qquad F(3,6) = 12.3031, \qquad DW = 2.4733$$

Whether the price variables were entered separately or in ratio form, it did not seem to alter the magnitude of the import price elasticity of approximately -12.5. However, it is rather remarkable to see such a large import price elasticity compared with those of the other groups. This might be due to the fact that there are more substitution possibilities for work shoes. Efforts at estimating the demand and supply for domestic work shoes have been futile.

The results for the athletic footwear group seem encouraging. The import demand equation on a per capita consumption basis has been estimated to be

(5e) $$\log q_m(\text{Ath}) = -54.6308 - 0.5760 \log \frac{p_{m_2}}{p_d} + 6.7219 \log y$$
$$\qquad\qquad\qquad\qquad (0.2523) \qquad\qquad (1.0363)$$
$$\qquad\qquad\qquad\qquad (2.2828)^* \qquad\qquad (6.4862)^*$$

$$R^2 = 0.9579, \qquad F(2,7) = 79.6751, \qquad DW = 2.3229$$

The import price elasticity is about -0.6, comparable to that of the M/B group and on the low side compared with other categories. Entering the price variables separately using the OLS and TSLS methods produced comparable results, as reported in equations (6e) and (7e) of Appendix Table III-E.

As for the demand for domestic athletic shoes, our attempts to estimate it have not met with much success, as shown by equation (8e) in Table III-E. Although the price elasticity of demand has the right sign and a reasonable magnitude, it is not statistically significant. However, as has been consistently true in other categories, the supply equation is the easier to identify statistically, and it appears as

(9e) $\log Q_s(\text{Ath}) = -2.8186 + 1.0292 \log \hat{p}_d$
                            (0.5492)
                            (1.8740)

          $R^2 = 0.2182,$ $F(1,8) = 3.512,$ $DW = 2.9541$

*(f)   Use of Italian Footwear Prices (p_{m_4}) as Proxy
       for Imported Footwear Prices*

When Italian footwear prices were used as proxy for imported footwear prices, we obtained elasticity coefficients at the sample means of -2 for import price elasticity, 3.8 for cross-elasticity, and 5.6 for income elasticity, as shown by

(1f) $\tilde{q}_m = -7.6604 + 0.0028y - 0.0264p_{m_4} + 0.0456p_d$
                    (0.0003) (0.0079) (0.0158)
                    $(10.0175)*$ $(-3.3099)*$ $(2.8899)*$
                    (5.6238) (-2.0055) (3.7712)
                                          elasticities at sample means
          $R^2 = 0.9789,$ $F(3,9) = 139.4,$ $DW = 2.0095$

When log values were used, however, the import price coefficient assumed the wrong sign.

Using Italian footwear prices in proxy form seems to have raised the import price elasticity estimate from -1.5 to -2.0, bringing our results closer to those of others (i.e., Simon's). However, Italian footwear prices did not fare very well in explaining women's footwear imports as much as men's. Again, note that Italian footwear represent only 40% of the total United States footwear imports and this is declining, which reduces our confidence in the above estimate.

*(g)   Effect of Cyclical Income Changes on the Demand
        for Imported and Domestic Shoes*

Finally, we attempted to measure the effect of cyclical income changes on imports and domestic demand to ascertain how the demand for shoes would be affected by recession. The results are presented in Appendix Table III-G.

The coefficient of unemployment in the total (composite) demand function including imports, as shown in equation (lg) of Appendix Table III-G, turned out to be negative; whereas it shows a positive sign in the import demand function, as shown by equations (2g) and (3g) in the table. This seems to imply that during the downturn of the cycle, footwear import demand would not decline as much as the total demand for footwear and, conversely, under the recovery phase of the cycle, imports would rise less rapidly than domestic footwear demand. When it comes to categories, only the M/B group yielded sensible results in that the unemployment term has a positive coefficient in conformity with the results of total imports and a negative coefficient in the demand equation for domestic footwear, as shown in equations (4g) and (5g) of Appendix Table III-G.

Summary

In general, the empirical results indicate that even though the United States demand for footwear is nearly perfectly price inelastic, the import demand for footwear exhibits much higher price elasticity, about -1.5. It is interesting to note that import price elasticity for the W/M group, estimated to be around -2, is much higher than that for M/B, which is put at -0.5. As to the domestic supply of footwear, all major categories demonstrate high price elasticities, averaging around 5.

Updating some of the important empirical results by including data for 1974 and 1975 has not appreciably changed our findings. In fact, the errors introduced by using faulty preliminary figures for 1975 turned up some nonsensical results.

3.   COST/BENEFIT ANALYSIS

In this section we develop calculations of the social costs of tariff restrictions on imported nonrubber footwear within the analytical framework previously detailed. Our parameter estimates in Section 2 indicate that the import price elasticity is about -1.5, which seems to be at variance with an unpublished finding of Wayne Simon of the ITC,[13] who suggests a much higher import price elasticity of -3.5. This latter magnitude is also closer to the average import price elasticity for imports in general.[14] However, a recent study by Price and Thornblade reports that import price elasticity of footwear from Italy is -2.6 and from Spain -1.3, which would give an average import price elasticity not too different from our own estimate.[15]

On the other hand, the price elasticity of demand for footwear seems to be close to zero or highly inelastic, which is in substantial agreement with other studies. The supply elasticity turned out to be quite high, about 5 or 6, which is also in accord with other independent estimates.[14, 16]

In our cost/benefit analysis to follow, we will provide the range of values from -1.5 to -3.5 for the import price elasticity. Also, in estimating the impact of increased imports on domestic sales, we will assume perfect domestic supply elasticity and, in addition, treat 100 pairs of imported as equivalent to 52 pairs of domestic shoes, since the average domestic shoe price is $6.41 while the average imported shoe price is $3.31 per pair as of 1973. In other words, in terms of efficiency units, 1 pair of domestic shoes is roughly equivalent to 2 pairs of imported shoes. The assumption of a high degree of substitutability between the two groups of shoes (imported and domestic), is made to

[13]Note that Simon used different price series data in that he used as a proxy for imported footwear the footwear WPI of Italy and Japan. The proportion of imports accounted for by these two countries in 1973 was 38%. In addition, quarterly data were utilized in his study, whereas ours were annual data. Price series were not deflated as they were in our study, and Simon's estimate concerns only aggregate import demand for footwear.

[14]Magee suggests that supply elasticity should be higher than demand elasticity. For example, the short-run domestic demand and supply elasticities for United States goods competing with imports are -0.25 and 0.50, respectively; while the long-run elasticities are -0.75 and 1.50 for demand and supply, respectively.

[15]However, a study by Price and Thornblade [64, pp. 46–57] reports that import price elasticity of footwear from Italy is -2.6 and from Spain -1.3. Unfortunately, their estimated price elasticity of imports from Japan turned out to have a positive sign with the magnitude of 1.2, which is implausible.

[14,16]Magee's import price elasticity is about -3 in the short run (5 years) and -8 in the long run. The short-run elasticities are consistent with those found in Houthakker and Magee [56, pp. 111–125], and the long-run elasticities are consistent with those of Floyd [53, pp. 95–107].

obtain the upper-limit estimate of the impact of imports on domestic sales. This is a reasonable assumption in view of the fact that the demand for total footwear (including imports) is almost completely inelastic, while the import demand is price elastic, suggesting that an increase in imports caused by falling import prices must necessarily replace purchases of domestic shoes. To the extent that these assumptions do not hold strictly, our estimates of costs due to resource reallocation would be overstated, which would make our calculations of net gains from tariff reduction conservative. Note also that the larger the import price elasticity, the greater the gains associated with a given tariff reduction. In our study, therefore, we hold to an import price elasticity of -1.5 as our best estimate, while allowing for the computation of an elasticity of -3.5.

Instead of assuming that two units of imported footwear displace one unit of domestic production, we tried to obtain statistically the displacement effect on domestic footwear production of an increase in imports due to a tariff reduction. To perform such a calculation, a regression equation for United States demand for domestic output of all shoes is needed. Ideally, the knowledge of the cross-elasticity of demand for domestic output with respect to import price would then allow us to estimate such a displacement effect. However, we were not successful in estimating the United States demand for domestic footwear, because all the estimated coefficients had wrong signs in the regressions using p_{m_1} (the unit-value index), as can be seen in equations (1h) and (2h) in Appendix Table III-H.

Returning to the explicit calculations of gains and losses, first the increase in consumer surplus given by area A' in Figure III-3a may be computed using the expression

$$A' = \frac{1}{2} t^2 \eta_m V_m$$

With $t = 0.10$ (roughly the weighted average tariff rate on imported footwear),[17] letting $\eta_m = -1.5$, and given a value of imported footwear V_m in 1973 of approximately \$900 million, we get $A' = \$6.75$ million. In other words, assuming the import price elasticity of demand equal to -1.5 and using the value of imported footwear in 1973, the net gain to

---

[17]In 1973 the tariff rates on various categories of footwear were M/B 8.5%, women's 15%, misses 10%, and vinyl footwear 6%. The corresponding value weights were 0.31, 0.41, 0.05, and 0.23. The weighted average tariff rate is therefore 10.69%.

society attributable to the increase in consumer surplus would be roughly $6.75 million annually, assuming for the moment no growth in import demand. On the other hand, if we use Simon's finding of $\eta_m = -3.5$, the revised estimate of the net gain from this source is about $16 million per year. As mentioned earlier, the calculations of the gains due to consumer surplus would be slightly overstated, since the ordinary rather than the compensated demand curve is used. The value of gains based upon an import price elasticity of -1.5 is $6.75 million, whereas it is $15.75 million when based on an import price elasticity of -3.5. The estimated gains from the 10% tariff reduction on imported footwear are based upon 1973 volume of imports.

The question arises as to the rate at which imports of shoes is expected to increase in the future. Since 1963, the value of footwear imports increased at the annual average rate of 32%, even though the import growth rate seemed to have peaked to an annual rate of 52% in 1968 and then gradually declined to around 15% in 1973. It is to be expected that as the share of imports increases in the domestic footwear market, the rate of growth in footwear imports will further slow down. Therefore, we cannot avoid an element of arbitrariness in projecting the rate of growth of footwear imports into the future, but we will make the assumption that it will grow proportionately with the increase in disposable income, as is the case with the total imports of goods and services for the United States. This would imply that the import demand curve will shift outwardly to the right at about 4% per annum in the foreseeable future, assuming that the rate of increase in income is of about the same magnitude. However, it should be recognized that the growth of footwear imports in the near future will not decelerate to such a low rate, whereas in the long run the rate of growth in imports might fall much below 4%. Note further that the United States demand for footwear in general has been growing at the annual rate of about 1% commensurate with the population growth rate, secularly. This, in turn, will tend to enlarge the net gain due to consumer surplus increase represented by area A' by about the same percentage each year. So, we need to compute the present value of the future stream of gains using the discount rate of 8% (from long-term United States Treasury Notes) and to subtract from it the present value of costs of resource reallocation, primarily with regard to labor displacement due to import penetration.

Now, the present value of the gains from freer trade in any given year i can be written as

$$PV_i = \frac{0.5t^2\eta_m V_m(1 + g)^i}{(1 + r)^i} = 0.5t^2\eta_m V_m(1 + d)^i$$

where

g = growth rate of imported footwear
r = discount rate
d = discount factor incorporating both growth and the
      rate of capitalization r, i.e., $d \simeq g - r$

which in our case comes out to be

$$PV_i = 0.5(0.10)^2\eta_m\$900,000,000(1 - 0.04)^i$$
$$= 0.005\eta_m\$900,000,000(0.96)^i$$

Therefore, the present value of the gains from removal of consumption
DWL, including growth, is the sum of all future discounted losses
discounted by a factor of 4%. Table III-1 not only gives the total present
gains of a 10% tariff reduction, but also breaks up the present value of
the gains into several time periods, giving the reader some feel for the
trajectory of the total present value. The calculations in Table III-1 show
that the present value of benefits declines, gradually summing up to the
total value of $162.20 million in the case of $\eta_m = -1.5$. For the case of η_m
$= -3.5$, the present value of benefits amounts to $378 million.

In subtracting the losses due to job changes resulting from trade
liberalization, we shall assume that the adjustment process is completed within 1 year, obviating the necessity for calculation of present
values. This is not an unreasonable assumption for an industry like
footwear, which is not capital-intensive. A recent publication of the
Public Research Institute (PRI) [98], which uses elaborate models of
converting output changes to employment changes in the United States
steel industry, estimates that employment adjustment to a change in
production is complete within six quarters.

Postulating a decline in sales of domestic shoes approximating
the increase in quantity imported and using $\eta_m = -1.5$, yields a decline
in value of domestic shoe sales of about $141.5 million.[18] Now the

---

[18]The latter was derived by assuming that the price elasticity of demand for
footwear in general is zero, whereas the price elasticity of demand for imported footwear
is -1.5. When the imported shoe price falls by 10%, the quantity demanded of imports
will increase by 15% or by 42.5 million pairs, which translates into a decrease in demand
of domestically produced footwear of 22.1 million pairs. Using the average price of $6.41
per pair of domestic shoes would amount to a decline in sales of about $141.5 million.

TABLE III-1

Time Path of the Present Value of Consumption
Dead-Weight Loss, 1973 (Million Dollars)

$$\eta_m = -1.5$$

$$PV_i^a = 0.005\eta_m\$900,000,000,000(0.96)^i$$

i	Present value of benefits	Present value of losses	Net benefit (+) or net loss (−)
1	6.48	−24.34[b]	17.86 (−)
2	6.22	−13.57	7.35 (−)
3	5.97	−12.67	6.70 (−)
4	5.73	−11.64	5.91 (−)
5	5.51	−3.16	2.35 (+)
1–5	29.91	−65.38	35.47 (−)
1–13	66.91	−83.51	16.77 (−)
1–18	84.36	−83.51	0.85 (+)
19–00	77.84	0	77.84 (+)
Total PV	162.20	−83.51	78.69

[a]$\Sigma PV = B_A(1 + 0.96 + 0.96^2 + 0.96^3 + \cdots + 0.96^n); \Sigma B_A/1 - 0.96 = B_A(1/0.04) =$
$B_A(25)$, where B_A is the increase in the annual flow of consumer surplus or benefits.

[b]The first year figure of $24.34 million was obtained by adding up the total wage loss by both the permanently displaced and temporarily displaced workers, including their wage reductions. From the second year until the thirteenth year, the present value of wage losses by the permanently displaced workers are added to the wage differential suffered by the reemployed workers. By the eighteenth year, the cost of $83.51 million to society from trade liberalization is completely offset by the gain to society, leaving a net gain to society of $78.69 million.

question arises as to how many workers will be displaced as a result of the cutback in domestic production. As a rough estimate, we can divide the total value of domestic footwear production—about $3 billion—by the total number of footwear workers—about 170,000—and arrive at a figure of $18,000 per worker per year. The latter figure corresponds to about fifty-five workers displaced for each $1 million cutback in domestic production.[19] Here, the average output–labor

---

This was derived by assuming that 100 pairs of imported shoes replace 52 pairs of domestic shoes on the average, since the average price for the former is $3.31 and for the latter $6.41. In other words, roughly 2 pairs of imported shoes are equivalent to 1 pair of domestically produced shoes in efficiency units.

[19]The Bureau of Labor Statistics in 1966 estimated that on the average 76,618 jobs are lost for each $1 billion cutback in production in import-competing industries. Law-

coefficient is used as an approximation to the marginal output–labor coefficient, which is not available. Traditionally, estimates of the impact of tariffs on employment have utilized the average labor productivity concept. The expected decline in domestic production is translated into an estimate of the labor displaced by imports by describing the labor required to produce said output, given the average labor productivity in the affected industry. However, as the PRI study indicates, this methodology may be subject to important limitations. For example, the method may lead to a significant overestimate of the net amount of labor displacement in that the potential offsets to tariff losses from industry growth or normal labor attrition are ignored. Also, if there are scale factors affecting industry labor productivity or differences in labor productivity between plants, obvious discrepancies will arise in applying the average approach. It should be recognized, however, that the foregoing method may still produce valid estimates. An industry such as shoes, producing under constant cost conditions and hiring labor at a competitive wage, as brought out in the structural survey of the industry, may still satisfy the basic conditions for the application of the average labor productivity concept.

Using the labor–output coefficient of 55 displaced workers for each $1 million cutback in domestic production ($141.5 million) gives 7781 workers displaced per year. The total cost due to job losses can be estimated along the lines suggested by McCarthy, who analyzed the trade adjustment experience of the Massachusetts shoe industry [31].[20]

Since it is found that 25.7% of the workers once displaced become permanently unemployed, the present value of their total wage loss for a typical worker has been estimated to be $18,024.85. This estimate is based on the fact that the average age of permanently displaced workers is 61.1 years; they will be unemployed until the average retirement age of 65; and this implies an average annual wage loss of $5183.88 for 3.9 years. The annual wage was computed from the weekly wage of $99.69 in 1975 dollars, which was adjusted for inflation (based upon the increase in the General Price Index) from McCarthy's estimate of $83.77 in 1973 dollars. An 8% discount rate was used as

---

rence Krause (1970–1971) estimates that each $1 billion of additional imports displaced 88,600 jobs. See [30, No. 2]. The marginal analysis of Krause is, of course, more relevant since policy issues deal with changes from current levels.

[20]Even though Massachusetts represents about 12% of United States production in pairage terms, it is representative of the Northeastern shoe-producing region, which accounts for over 50% of United States production.

before. In addition, it has been found that even the displaced worker who gets rehired remains unemployed for 18.2 weeks on the average. Furthermore, his new wage is permanently lower than the preimpact wage rate ($106.16) for this group by 11.3%, which amounts to $12.00 per week, or $624 per year. When this figure is adjusted for inflation, it amounts to $742.56. Then, the present value of the total loss of such a worker is made up of the wages lost during the unemployment period, namely $2299.21, which has been adjusted for inflation and the present value of the wage differential until retirement ($5893.01) making for a total lifetime loss of $8192.22 in 1975 dollars. This estimate is based upon the fact that the average age of reemployed workers is 51.6 years, with the retirement age of 65 years.

Using $\eta_m = -1.5$, a 10% reduction in the tariff rate results in 7781 workers being displaced. Then, the present value aggregate wage loss suffered by those 2000 workers who are permanently unemployed is $36.1 million. The corresponding figure for those 5781 workers who are temporarily displaced amounts to $47.4 million. Therefore, the total labor displacement cost caused by trade liberalization will be $83.5 million. On the other hand, using the high value of $\eta_m = -3.5$ would give as the total amount of wages lost to be about $194.6 million, which is greater by a factor of 2.33.

To compute the net gains or losses to society resulting from a postulated 10% tariff reduction on footwear, the costs of reallocation incurred by the displaced labor[21] have to be subtracted from the gains. These are shown in the fourth column of Table III-1 and indicate a net gain of $78.69 million in 1975 dollars. (For the high elasticity of -3.5, this would amount to $183.61 million.) It is obvious that losses to society outweigh the gains for the first 17 years, but are more than made up during the eighteenth and the succeeding years. As discussed earlier, if we are to estimate the consumer dead-weight loss stemming from a further increase in the tariff rate, say, double the current level, it would be approximately quadrupled, implying that our estimate of the loss of net social benefit would have to be put at $648 million instead of

[21]Estimating the loss due to capital displacement, while theoretically similar to that of labor, poses practical difficulties. If the capital stock displaced from production on removal of tariffs is liquid, it will readily move into other investment alternatives. For fixed capital, unless there is an alternative use for its utilization, the loss to society will be the value of the capital less its scrap value. Since most small firms—that is, the firms particularly vulnerable to import competition—lease their equipment and machinery, the owners of these machines might find it easier to export them.

$162.2 million minus the displacement cost of $83.51 million. Here, the case against further increases in the tariff rate on economic grounds alone becomes much stronger.

Turning to the analysis of noncompeting footwear groups and assuming that the same elasticities hold in each group (so that intergroup comparisons can be made), we may calculate the net gains to society from a 1% tariff reduction in each category of footwear by simply allocating the net gains associated with the tariff reduction in the particular category, based upon its relative importance in value terms. The assumption of equal elasticities, even though at odds with our empirical findings, is made as a first approximation.

For the M/B group, which accounts for approximately 30% of the total value of imported footwear, the total present value of net gains associated with a 1% tariff reduction would be equal to one-tenth the total present value of net gains for the entire group of footwear imports multiplied by the percentage of M/B footwear imports in that total. When $\eta_m = -1.5$, this would amount to ($78.69/10)0.30 = $2.36 million, approximately, whereas when $\eta_m = -3.5$, the amount would be $2.36 million $\times$ (3.5/1.5) = $5.51 million. For the W/M group, which accounts for 57% of the total imports in value terms, the corresponding amount ranges between $4.49 and $10.46 million. For the C/I group, which accounts for only 3% of total imports, the net gains would range between $0.24 and $0.56 million. However, if the estimated $\eta_m = -0.5$ for M/B is used, the net gains to society resulting from a 10% reduction in the tariff rate would lead to $7.87 million; while for W/M, with a much higher import price elasticity of -2, the net gains would be a substantially larger $59.80 million.

4.   CONCLUDING REMARKS

In this chapter, we have investigated the probable impact of tariff restrictions on imported footwear for the United States footwear industry as imports of shoes have grown rapidly over the past 10 years, capturing an increasing share of the domestic market. It seems obvious even to the casual observer that most of the increase in domestic demand for footwear has been met by imports, while the industry has suffered in terms of reduced sales, employment, etc.

Our empirical findings indicate that based upon the estimated import price elasticity of -1.5, the elimination of the current 10% tariff rate would increase imports by approximately 15%, while another study puts the elasticity estimate as high as -3.5, which would increase imports by 35%. However, Price and Thornblade's estimate [64] of import price elasticity is much closer to ours. On the other hand, the price elasticity of demand for footwear in general appears to be nearly perfectly inelastic, in conformity with other studies. Then, our findings indicate that the elimination of the current tariff will confer total consumer welfare gains ranging from $162.2 to $377.9 million, based upon the assumption of 4% increase in demand for imported footwear and a social rate of discount of 8%, whereas costs of approximately $83.51–$194.6 million in the form of lost earnings by displaced workers, are more than offset by the gains within 13 years. In other words, the net social gains resulting from the tariff reduction would be $78.69 million for our import price elasticity estimate of -1.5 and $183.61 million for the alternative estimate of -3.5. This clearly indicates that the gains to society as a whole associated with the given tariff reduction will more than compensate for any loss incurred by affected groups. That is, the "gainers" can easily compensate the "losers," implying that adjustment assistance to the injured workers and firms out of the general tax revenue would be justified on economic grounds alone.

Our calculations of gains from tariff reduction would, of course, be overstated if there are terms-of-trade effects, in that an increase in imports brought about by trade liberalization would also raise the foreign price of imported footwear, because of the upward-sloping foreign supply curve. However, since shoes are light manufactured products, it seems plausible that supply is highly elastic in the world market, making the terms-of-trade effects minimal.

Looking at the two major groups by sheer volume of sales, coupled with the much higher import price elasticity than that for M/B footwear, tariff restrictions on women's shoes would tend to inflict a much larger social cost relative to the M/B group. On the other hand, those on children's footwear and special-purpose footwear such as athletic, work, and slippers would not.

Finally, our estimates of consumer gains do not include such intangibles as a greater range of choice open to consumers afforded by greater variety, styles, and comfort available in the import mix. Neither do our estimates of losses resulting from unemployment include the possible psychological and social costs to the affected individuals, such as the impact of unemployment on physical and mental illness, mortality rates, deterioration of family relations, etc.

APPENDIX TO CHAPTER III

Construction of the Weighted Import Price Index for Footwear

In each group, the weighted price index (p_{m2}) was obtained by weighting seven digit TSUSA items and averaging them:

$$P_{mj} = \sum_i W_{ij} P_i$$

j = men/boys, women/misses, children/infants, athletic, work, slippers, others

i = all the TSUSA items to be included in the jth category

$\sum W_{ij} = 1$

W_{ij} = $\dfrac{\text{value of imports of } i\text{th TSUSA item of } j\text{th category}}{\text{value of imports of } j\text{th category}}$

In choosing value weights for the import price index for each group, the sample period was bifurcated into two subperiods, 1964–1967 and 1968–1973. In the first subperiod, 1964–1967, the frequent annual changes in TSUSA classifications necessitated the use of separate value weights for each year, whereas for the second subperiod, 1968 was used as a base year since the TSUSA items remain uniform thereafter.

The basic Work Sheet of data utilized in the construction of this index is not included in this report, since it would merely contribute bulk to the report. However, it is available for examination upon request.

TABLE III-A

Equation number	Form	Dependent variable	Intercept	p_c	y	p_m	p_d	p_m/p_d
1a	OLS	$\bar{q}_c$	5.0213	−0.4749 (0.1679) (−2.8218)*	+0.2773 (0.3528) (0.7860)			
2a	OLS	$\bar{q}_m$	−53.7314		+5.2199 (0.3684) (14.1698)*	−1.3045† (0.1403) (−9.2980)*	+4.1223 (1.2666) (3.2546)*	
3a	OLS	$\bar{q}_m$	−44.7154		+6.6081 (0.4102) (16.1089)			−1.4017† (0.2391) (−5.8626)*
4a	OLS	$\bar{q}_m$	−37.6599		+5.3602 (0.3940) (13.6028)*			−1.2098† (0.1493) (−8.1027)*
5a	OLS	$\bar{q}_m$	−62.2637		+4.8135 (0.5542) (8.6860)*	−1.5804† (0.2701) (−5.1766)*	+6.9919 (1.3507) (5.1766)*	
6a	OLS	$\bar{q}_m$	−43.9203		+6.6815 (0.4108) (16.2624)*			−1.7416† (0.3771) (−4.6180)*
7a	OLS	v_m	−33.6587					−1.0574† (0.7368) (−1.4350)
8a	OLS	P_m†	247.8020					
9a	TSLS	$\bar{Q}_s$	−4.4424					

				Y	P_W	Q_m	P_d	Population
7a	OLS	v_m	−33.6587	+4.1807 (2.0689) (2.0207)*	+1.2159 (5.3436) (0.2275)			
8a	OLS	P_m†	247.8020	+13.0550 (12.8327) (1.0170)	−8.3291 (7.9096) (1.0530)	−0.4840 (0.9379) (0.5158)	+5.6090 (3.1063) (1.8060)	−75.8012 (49.3849) (1.5350)

^{a}The first set of numbers in parentheses indicate the standard errors of the regression coefficients; the second set of numbers in parentheses indicate the t values; * denotes significant at the 5% level; † indicates that p_{m_1}, the simple unit-value index, was used in the regression; ‡ indicates that p_{m_2}, the weighted unit-value index, was used in the regression. This arrangement will hold uniformly for all tables reporting regression results.

Regression Coefficients (All in Logs) for Total United States Footwear Market[a]

t	$\hat{p}_\mathrm{d}$	p_ℓ	w	c_u	R^2	Degrees of freedom	F	DW
					0.5444	2,7	4.19	1.9258
					0.9918	3,14	565.68	0.9908
					0.9659	2,16	226.81	0.5505
					0.9892	2,15	687.05	0.7042
+0.1607 (0.0932) (1.7239)					0.9853	4,14	234.80	1.0094
+0.1522 (0.1315) (1.1575)					0.9867	3,15	154.87	0.8458
					0.8550	3,15	29.47	1.0946
					0.9456	5,5	17.37	2.5959
	+4.5645 (1.2793) (3.5678)*	−0.7329 (0.6013) (−1.2187)	−2.4697 (0.6946) (−3.5554)*		0.6908	3,14	10.43	1.7171

95

TABLE III-B

Equation number	Form	Dependent variable	Intercept	p_c	y	p_d	p_m	p_m/p_d
1b	OLS	$\tilde{q}_c$	2.6813	−0.2183 (0.1442) (−1.5139)m	+0.3819 (0.3400) (0.1124)			
2b	OLS	q_m	−41.3407		+4.3456 (0.9691) (4.4838)*	+1.9678 (2.3584) (0.8344)	−0.3469† (0.2043) (−1.6979)m	
3b	OLS	q_m	−37.3562		+4.9817 (0.3221) (15.4634)*			−0.3275† (0.1978) (−1.6553)m
4b	OLS	q_m	−34.0770		+4.7312 (0.4769) (9.9188)*			−0.6407† (0.4766) (−1.3444)
5b	OLS	q_m	−39.2619		+4.3337 (1.0083) (4.2978)*	+1.7575 (2.4933) (0.7008)	−0.5786† (0.5112) (−1.2229)m	
6b	OLS	q_m	−38.7411		+4.5989 (1.7687) (2.5945)*	+0.9873 (3.2472) (0.3041)	−0.5791‡ (1.4304) (−0.4058)	
7b	OLS	q_m	−35.0661		+4.7574 (0.5757) (8.2635)*			−0.6757† (0.9892) (−0.6831)
8b	OLS	q_m	−40.1835		+4.3119 (1.7178) (2.5099)*	+1.7007 (3.6652) (0.4640)	−0.4965‡ (0.9669) (−0.5135)	
9b	OLS	q_m	−36.2292		+4.8357 (0.6443) (7.5053)*			−0.5451‡ (0.8190) (−0.6656)
10b	OLS	q_m	−47.7186		+5.1398 (1.8410) (2.7919)*	+3.2680 (3.0797) (1.0612)	−1.8534‡ (1.9269) (−0.9618)	
11b	OLS	q_m	−53.7297		+4.7475 (1.0835) (2.7919)*	+7.0552 (2.8223) (2.4999)*	−3.6892‡ (1.3275) (−2.7792)*	
12b	OLS	q_m	−31.4598		+5.8895 (0.6441) (9.1440)*			−3.4014‡ (1.1833) (−2.8744)*
13b	TSLS	q_m	−40.9011		+3.9410 (2.0826) (1.9035)	+2.2980 (3.9718) (0.5786)	−0.3587‡ (1.4971) (−0.2386)	
14b	TSLS	q_d	8.0368		+0.0846 (0.8478) (0.0997)		−0.1112‡ (0.4835) (−0.2301)	
15b	TSLS	$\tilde{Q}_s$	−13.9056					
16b	TSLS	$\tilde{Q}_s$	−24.9690					

[a]See footnote [a] to Table III-A.

Regression Coefficients (All in Logs) for M/B[a]

t	$\hat{p}_d$	p_ℓ	w	c_u	R^2	Degrees of freedom	F	DW
					0.2489	2,7	1.16	1.4775
					0.9741	3,10	125.6	1.0722
					0.9728	2,11	196.56	1.2407
+0.0881 (0.1213) (0.7259)					0.9741	3,10	125.58	1.1637
+0.0667 (0.1351) (0.4936)					0.9747	4,9	86.83	1.0391
					0.9070	3,6	19.54	0.945
					0.9070	2,7	34.14	0.968
					0.912	3,6	20.75	0.899
					0.911	2,7	35.69	0.972
					0.924	3,5	20.16	1.391
					0.963	3,5	42.74	2.7711
					0.953	2,6	61.23	2.7200
	+2.2980 (3.9718) (0.5786)				0.905	3,6	18.96	0.904
	−1.7111 (1.6977) (−1.0078)m				0.6411	3,6	3.57	1.548
	+6.4528 (2.2757) (2.8355)*	−0.2552 (0.2888) (−0.8833)	−3.0384 (1.3247) (−2.2937)*		0.6755	3,10	12.67	1.6058
	+6.5537 (2.2685) (2.8889)*	−0.0095 (0.0289) (−0.3287)	−2.8726 (1.2544) (−2.2899)*	+2.3498 (1.9953) (1.1776)m	0.3795	4,9	1.38	2.0611

TABLE III-C

Equation number	Form	Dependent variable	Intercept	p_c	y	p_d	p_m	p_m/p_d
1c	OLS	$\tilde{q}_c$	5.0214	+0.2773 (0.3528) (0.7859)	−0.4739 (0.1679) (−2.8218)*			
2c	OLS	q_m	−64.9431		+8.2658 (0.4607) (17.9411)*	+6.4056 (1.2554) (5.1026)*	−1.9648† (0.1621) (−12.1200)*	
3c	OLS	q_m	−51.0823		+9.1143 (0.5503) (16.5618)*			−2.1179† (0.2208) (−9.5911)*
4c	OLS	q_m	−36.3816		+5.5923 (1.0253) (5.4542)*			−0.7239† (0.2067) (−3.5029)*
5c	OLS	q_m	−37.5208		+3.3064 (0.4796) (6.8941)*	+1.6841 (1.1113) (1.5155)	+0.8831‡ (0.4920) (1.7951)	
6c	OLS	q_m	−29.2528		+2.5978 (0.7004) (3.7090)*			+1.9520 (0.6195) (3.1511)*
7c	TSLS	q_d	22.6328		−1.8784 (0.7373) (−2.5473)*		+5.1501 (0.8038) (0.6408)	
8c	TSLS	Q_s	−14.3177					
9c	TSLS	Q_s	−14.2123					

[a]See footnote [a] to Table III-A.

Regression Coefficients (All in Logs) for W/M[a]

t	$\hat{p}_d$	p_ℓ	w	k_n	c_u	R^2	Degrees of freedom	F	DW
						0.5444	2,7	4.18	1.9258
						0.9814	3,10	229.3	1.6678
						0.9629	2,11	169.6	0.9217
+0.3392 (0.2074) (1.6355)						0.9855	3,10	227.3	1.1310
						0.9860	3,6	140.7	2.1536
						0.9574	2,7	78.7	1.9401
	−1.9920 (1.9091) (−1.0435)					0.8192	3,6	8.133	1.638
	+5.2303 (1.7775) (2.9425)*	−0.3061 (0.4611) (−0.6638)	−3.7846 (0.9459) (−4.0012)*			0.8192	3,6	8.925	1.8247
	+5.5214 (0.9762) (5.6568)*	−0.5575 (0.3079) (−1.8104)*	−4.3970 (0.6371) (−6.9021)*	+0.2451 (0.1384) (1.7709)*		0.8920	4,5	19.65	2.0414

TABLE III-I

Equation number	Form	Dependent variable	Intercept	p_d	p_m	y
1d	OLS	q_m	−62.9736	+3.4745 (1.6898) (2.0561)*	−1.0742‡ (0.8184) (−1.3174)	+6.4541 (0.8297) (7.7785)*
2d	OLS	q_m	−53.1229			+7.2361 (0.7541) (9.5954)*
3d	TSLS	q_m	−63.3411		−1.1188‡ (0.8241) (−1.3577)	+6.4174 (0.8358) (7.6781)*
4d	TSLS	q_d	38.047		−4.0893‡ (13.2368)	−1.0899 (13.4291)
5d	TSLS	Q_s	−7.0328		(−0.3089)	(−0.0812)

[a]See footnote [a] to Table III-A.

Regression Coefficients (All in Logs) for CI[a]

$\hat{p}_d$	w	p_l	p_m/p_d	R^2	d.f.	F	DW
				0.952	3,6	39.71	1.97
			−1.0647	0.930	2,7	47.14	2.064
			(0.9064)				
			(−1.1745)				
+3.6624				0.952	3,6	39.62	1.94
(1.7575)							
(2.0839)*							
−2.3060				0.062	3,6	0.132	2.81
(28.1537)							
(−0.0819)							
+3.8226	−0.8057	−3.9063		0.951	3,6	27.79	3.013
(0.9660)	(0.1781)	(0.7247)					
(3.9570)*	(−4.5239)*	(−5.3904)*					

TABLE III-E

Equation number	Form	Dependent	Intercept	p_m/p_d	y	$\hat{p}_d$	p_l
1e	OLS	q_m(Slp)	−32.3027	−0.9072‡ (0.2625) (−3.4555)*	+4.2660 (0.9251) (+4.6113)*		
2e	TSLS	Q_s(Slp)	− 1.3657			+2.5887 (1.1569) (2.2375)*	−0.7442 (0.6247) (−1.1912)*
3e	OLS	q_m(Wk)	− 5.4403		+4.8845 (5.4914) (0.8895)		
4e	OLS	q_m(Wk)	49.6974	−12.7830‡ (4.9670) (−2.5736)*	+0.5920 (2.9977) (0.1975)		
5e	OLS	q_m(Ath)	−54.6308	−0.5760‡ (0.2523) (−2.2828)*	+6.7219 (1.0363) (6.4862)*		
6e	OLS	q_m(Ath)	−42.1366		+5.2912 (2.5926) (2.0409)*		
7e	TSLS	q_m(Ath)	−41.6879		+5.2619 (2.7744) (1.8966)		
8e	TSLS	q_d(Ath)	56.4863		+5.2175 (3.1724) (1.6447)	−0.9187 (1.2244) (−0.7503)	
9e	TSLS	Q_s(Ath)	−2.8186			+1.0292 (0.5492) (1.8740)	

[a]See footnote [a] to Table III-A.

Regression Coefficients (All in Logs) for Other Footwear[a]

w	k_n	p_m	p_d	R^2	d.f.	F	DW
				0.7543	2,7	10.74	1.8092
$(-1.8469$	-0.2548			0.6397	4,5	4.995	2.1285
(1.2413)	(0.1036)						
$(-1.4879)^*$	$(-2.4593)^*$						
		$-12.4294\ddagger$	$+4.3299$	0.8602	3,6	12.3031	2.4733
		(5.0493)	(10.3219)				
		$(2.4616)^*$	(0.4195)				
				0.8410	2,7	8.5081	2.4461
				0.9579	2,7	79.6751	2.3229
		$-1.3687\ddagger$	$+0.4866$	0.9604	3,6	48.540	2.310
		(1.3314)	(0.3021)				
		(-1.0280)	(1.6109)				
		$-1.3960\ddagger$	$+0.4662$	0.9504	3,6	48.502	2.276
		(1.6171)	(0.7491)				
		(-0.8633)	(0.6224)				
		$-3.1696\ddagger$		0.4766	3,6	1.821	2.835
		(2.0976)					
		(-1.5111)					
				0.2182	1,8	3.512	2.9541

TABLE III-

Equation number	Form	Dependent	Intercept	p_c	p_d	u
1g	OLS	$q_c(T)$	1.2896	−0.4137 (0.5678) (0.7286)		−0.083 (0.6630) (0.6760)
2g	OLS	$q_m(T)$	−63.8385		+6.5350 (1.0108) (6.4657)*	+0.6789 (0.1655) (4.103)*
3g	OLS	$q_m(T)$	−47.2097			+0.6798 (0.2706) (2.5118)
4g	TSLS	$q_d(M/B)$	11.4852			−0.5019 (0.1465) (3.4269)
5g	TSLS	$q_d(M/B)$	9.7572			−0.4452 (0.1327) (3.3530)

    [a]See footnote [a] to Table III-A.

TABLE III-

Equation number	Form	Dependent variable	Intercept	$\hat{p}_d$	y
1h	OLS (levels)	$\bar{q}_d$	16.6920		−0.0037 (0.0006) (−5.8330)* (−0.6842)e
2h	TSLS (logs)	$\bar{q}_d$	5.6305	+0.5469 (0.3111) (1.7578)	0.6821 (0.1096) (−6.221)*

[a]See footnote [a] to Table III-A.
[b]el indicates the elasticity value at the sample means.

gression Coefficients Including the Unemployment Rate (All in Logs)[a]

y	p_{m_1}/p_d	p_{m_1}	$\hat{p}_d$	R^2	d.f.	F	DW
+0.4482 (0.0794) (−1.0493)				0.66	3,6	3.90	2.662
+4.968 (0.4203) (11.818)*		−1.2270 (0.1309) (−9.3777)*		0.9917	4,14	416.156	1.3346
+6.7919 (0.3634) (18.6940)*	−1.4013 (0.2067) (6.7787)*			0.9761	3,15	204.117	0.6764
+2.884 (0.6587) (4.379)*		+0.4150 (0.1344) (3.0873)*	−7.159 (1.6998) (4.2117)*	0.7082	4,9	5.459	1.5967
+2.4574 (0.5243) (4.6868)*		+0.3679 (0.1233) (2.9848)*	−6.0278 (1.3361) (4.5114)*	0.7297	4,9	6.0743	1.2839

gression Coefficients Including 1974 and 1975 Data Using p_{m_1}, 1960–1975
(Total United States Footwear Market)[a]

p_d	p_{m_1}	R^2	F	DW
+0.0696 (0.0464) (1.3120) (0.5094)el	−0.0007 (0.0074) (−0.0982) (−0.0071)el	0.7247	14.91	0.5963
	−0.0477 (0.0697) (−0.6851)	0.6724	16.49	0.6724

IV

TRADE ADJUSTMENT ASSISTANCE AND IMPORT COMPETITION

1. HISTORY AND EVOLUTION

The problem of trade adjustment assistance is a relatively recent phenomenon with no strong theoretical underpinning. Still, it has fostered a substantial and expanding literature, aimed at the revision of traditional trade theory, which assumed away the problem of adjustment and associated costs. Empirical studies dealing with the effects of United States restrictions on trade suggest significant welfare losses for American consumers resulting from such restrictions. Stephen Magee, for example, suggests that import restrictions cost American consumers some $18.3 billion in 1972 [30, p. 700]. C. Fred Bergsten suggests that the real losses are even greater when factors like scale economies and monopoly effects are taken into account [13, pp. 119–141]. John Floyd has presented detailed calculations of such costs, approaching an order of magnitude of $5.3 billion in 1973 [22, pp. 148–160].[1]

---

[1]This lower estimate is due in large part to the fact that, unlike Magee, Floyd did take into account the terms of trade effects of trade restrictions.

Even on a micro level, these costs appear to be quite significant. In the footwear industry, for example, the Federal Reserve Board estimated that H.R., the so-called "Mills Bill" would have added almost $2 billion to consumer costs for footwear alone, raising the average shoe price some 32% and particularly affecting lower-income groups [15, pp. 17–19]. Our own estimates in this study are not greatly at variance with those reported above.

To be sure, Congress has always recognized that certain segments of the economy could be adversely affected by changing conditions in international trade and had to determine what sort of remedies should be applied whenever injury due to import competition occurred. Prior to the enactment of the Trade Expansion Act (TEA) of 1962, the President's major weapon was the escape clause permitted by Article XIX of the General Agreement on Tariffs and Trade (GATT), which provided for tariff and/or quota relief. Subsequent, intervening legislation, such as the Trade Agreement Extension Act of 1951, further refined the language of the escape clause and empowered the Tariff Commission to conduct such investigations upon application by a representative of an injured industry [46, pp. 1332–1333].

Quite apart from the problem of determining when injury occurred or threatened, use of the escape clause was an open invitation to retaliation on the part of other countries and a worsening of both the trade and foreign relations of the United States. The shortcomings of the escape clause as a protectionist device are well known and are only briefly detailed here:

1.   It produces adverse economic and political consequences. That is, when escape clause action is contemplated or taken, trading partners retaliate by withdrawing concessions or by demanding alternate tariff benefits that are less favorable.

2.   It is a deterrent to trade agreements, in the sense that countries have at times been reluctant to sign new trade agreements with the United States, since they feel that such agreements may be abrogated by the escape clause.

3.   It requires proof of serious industrywide injury, and relief for firms and groups of workers is made contingent upon such industrywide injury.

4.   It provides inadequate remedies, since tariff increases and quota restraints are not the most suitable remedies to the problems of individual firms and groups of workers.

The antecedents of adjustment assistance are to be found in numerous legislative proposals of the 1950s but they only achieved policy significance under Title III of the TEA of 1962. David McDonald, President of the United Steelworkers Union, first focused public attention on the issue in 1954, when as a member of the Commission on Foreign Economic Policy (Randall Commission), he proposed that import-injured companies, communities, and workers be made eligible to receive government assistance [49, pp. 2–3].[2] The adoption of adjustment assistance in the United States was also inspired by foreign governments' programs, including those related to economic integration in Europe, although at present, only the United States and Canada have programs that specifically tie adjustment assistance to import injury [4, p. 111].

The TEA of 1962 was the first piece of American legislation to provide for adjustment assistance to firms and workers injured by import competition.[3] Rather than rely on the escape clause as a remedy to injured industries, the TEA provided for a program of adjustment assistance directly to firms and/or groups of workers, regardless of whether injury was applicable to the respective entities or to the industry as a whole. Firms injured by imports could apply for low-cost federal loans, technical assistance, and tax relief, while workers could receive adjustment allowances during a specified period of time, retraining, and relocation grants. In this way, the TEA presented the first opportunity for individual firms and groups of workers to petition for relief on their own, without proof of injury to their respective industry as a whole. Individual assistance, therefore, appeared to be a more realistic approach to the problem than tariff restrictions, since not every firm in a given industry will be adversely affected by imports at the same time. In addition, the disturbing effects of international trade restrictions may be skirted, and consumers at large may score a net gain on several grounds. For one, the prices of imported goods will not rise in the absence of trade restrictions and the range of choice open to consumers may be significantly enlarged. Low-income consumers, in particular, would gain the most, since they are particularly sensitive to price increases and because low-priced goods from abroad are the usual targets of United States import restrictions.[4]

---

[2] For additional specialized papers, see Commission on International Trade and Investment [19].

[3] Similar provisions are contained in the Trade Act of 1974 [95].

[4] This is due to the fact that internationally traded goods weigh more heavily in the

Experience with adjustment assistance under the TEA has produced mixed results. In the first 7 years since its inception (1962–1969) petitioning firms and workers were generally unsuccessful in their attempts to secure assistance. A mere $18.5 million had been authorized for the program by the end of 1972, and only half of this amount was actually allocated [27, p. 4]. In its operative period since 1970, some assistance has in fact been provided to petitioning firms and workers.[5]

A number of reasons have been advanced for this slow start of the program. It may well be that economic units were not aware of the law and, hence, were ignorant of its provisions for assistance. Many "Kennedy Rounds" tariff reductions actually took place between 1963 and 1972, and it was thus only in 1970–1971 that firms began to feel the real effects of these concessions [45, p. 52]. Also, injured parties may have been discouraged by the negative experience of others; and business and labor support for a more liberal trade policy may have weakened [23]. Last, but not least, a major cause of this apparent inactivity probably lies in the lengthy and complex procedure for determining eligibility and the stringent criteria which govern same. We now turn to a detailed examination of these criteria, since they are at the heart of the program.

Section 301 of the TEA lists four conditions that must be met before a firm or worker is eligible to apply for adjustment assistance, or an industry is eligible to apply for tariff relief. These conditions are the same as those required for industrywide relief under escape clause action.

1. Imports of a product like or directly competitive with an article produced by the petitioning firm (or workers) must be increasing.

This determination has been generally accomplished with not too much difficulty. Once it is established that imported products are

---

consumption stream of low-income consumers and because tariff rates appear to be higher on lower-quality goods, which are purchased more frequently by low-income groups [52].

[5] It should be interesting to examine the experience of adjustment assistance by attempting to explain the break in the decision pattern about 1969—pre-1969 no affirmative findings; post-1969 numerous affirmative findings, probably due to the appointment of commissioners having different philosophy—an indication that the law is rather loosely worded and gives the Tariff Commission ample variance. This comparative analysis, however, is beyond the scope of our research at the present time.

substitutes for those produced by the petitioning firm(s) or workers, it is sufficient to observe whether imports have increased over time. In making this determination, the Tariff Commission[6] usually considers only absolute increases in import levels and requires that an imported item show a definite upward trend. At times, however, the Commission has also considered the ratio of imports to domestic consumption, to get at a more complete picture of any reported import penetration.

Even the apparently simple language of this first requirement, however, is not completely free of difficulty. For example, Bale [12; 44, pp. 135–137; 45, p. 55] has pointed out a number of times in the literature that the interpretation of the term "directly competitive" is not at all clearcut. Indeed, recognizing the difficulty, the Commission itself has divided on this very issue a number of times, mostly in cases involving footwear. Bale convincingly shows how, by defining shoes in general into narrow and specific TSUSA classes, it is always possible to find a class where imports have not increased, although imports of shoes in total may have increased significantly [44, p. 136]. As a possible way out, Bale suggests the application of the theoretical concept of the elasticity of substitution to a given set of imported and domestic goods to determine if they are directly competitive. The practical limitations of this procedure, however, are quickly recognized and acknowledged as not viable under present constraints [44, p. 137].

> 2. The increased imports are in major part the result of trade concessions granted under trade agreements.

As a first step in determining whether there is a relationship between trade concessions and imports, the petitioner must show that the concessions were granted before the rise in imports took place. Two problems immediately surface. The first problem is to determine which are the relevant concessions. If a firm(s)/workers claim injury due to increased imports in 1970–1974, for example, can this current injury be linked to a trade concession that was granted in 1934? Or, should the relevant trade concession be one that was granted closer in time to the current period of increased imports? The legislative history of the TEA seems to indicate that it views the aggregate of all concessions granted since 1934 and has consistently—although not always

[6] Henceforth called simply "Commission." Under Section 171 of the Trade Act of 1974, the Tariff Commission was renamed as the United States International Trade Commission [91].

unanimously—considered the total reductions since the beginning of the trade agreements program, not necessarily only the most recent concessions granted.[7] Commissioners who have disagreed with the aggregation rule, have considered the effect of only the more recent concessions, while treating earlier reductions as "conditions of trade." They have asserted, in effect, that concessions granted years or even decades before imports increased have become part of the totality of market conditions and cannot be singled out as the major cause of increased imports. In a number of deliberations on women's footwear, for example, the fact that shoe imports were increasing before tariff concessions were granted was found to be sufficient evidence for the Commission to rule that the trade concessions had not induced the increased imports [89]. A further report on nonrubber footwear [88] resulted in a divided finding, with some commissioners asserting that the time lag between the concessions and the increased imports was too long to have any relevance, and that even the Kennedy Rounds reductions that began in 1968 were irrelevant because imports increased sharply prior to that date. Rather, attention was called to the disparity between United States and foreign wage rates, limited gains in American productivity, and rapid United States price increases, all of which were held to be of greater importance than tariff reductions [88].

A second, related problem, demands a show of causality between increased imports and trade concessions. Clearly, only a statistical test can provide an indication of such causality. The *Transmission Towers* [96] and *Buttweld Pipe* [85] cases show up the difficulty in proving a cause-and-effect relationship between trade concessions and increased imports, and the extent to which the concessions were the most significant causal factor. The Commission, aware of the difficulty, made a clever change in procedure. Instead of attempting to prove that tariff reductions were in major part responsible for increased imports, the Commission substituted what has become known as the "but for" test. It concluded in *Buttweld Pipe* that "we need ask ourselves only whether, but for the concessions, would imports be substantially at their present level" [85, p. 10].

The "but for" test may be interpreted in the following way: If, in

[7] The phrase "result of trade concessions granted under trade agreements" means the aggregate reduction that has been arrived at by means of a trade agreement or trade agreements (whether entered into under Section 201 of this bill (TEA) or under Section 350 of the Tariff Act of 1930 [92].

the absence of trade concessions, imports would not have increased, then the "in major part" provision would be met. More formally, trade concessions may be the cause of increased imports if the occurrence of concessions is sufficient for the subsequent occurrence of increased imports. This would imply that whenever concessions are granted, increased imports follow in quick succession. The astounding implication is that a given concession must immediately induce a rise in imports, to be followed by immediate complaint from the industry. If there is a delayed reaction, the "major part" causal link between concessions and increased imports cannot be supported [46, p. 1342]. In addition, to test the stated hypothesis, all other independent variables would have to be held constant, while trade concessions would represent the experimental variable.

To be sure, in the more recent period, the Commission has recognized that the chain of events indicated is not likely to be instantaneous [25, 36]. Normally, the physical plant in the exporting countries must be expanded to meet the increased demand caused by tariff reductions and a time lag between the two events should realistically be expected.

All in all, this second criterion has been appropriately called the "Achilles' heel" of the TEA [45, p. 66]. The Commission appears to have made the causal link between trade concessions and increased imports, an impossible burden of proof.

3. The firm is seriously injured, or threatened with serious injury (or in the case of workers, a significant number or portion of the petitioning workers are unemployed or underemployed or are threatened with unemployment or underemployment).

On the whole, this requirement has not been difficult to meet. Out of 131 cases presented through 1971, only six have failed to substantiate serious injury [45, p. 68]. Whether the industry, firm, or workers are seriously injured is an undeniable fact demonstrated by the evidence presented at the hearings. In the footwear industry, for example, all recent evidence involving falling domestic production, frequency of plant closings, and imports at about one-third of domestic consumption, would seem to indicate that competitive injury has occurred and that it may well increase in the future. It is equally true, however, that the Commission has also insisted on examining the importance of factors other than imports before making its determination and, in a scattered number of cases, has found that imports were not the major factor in causing or threatening serious injury.[8]

4. The increased imports (resulting in major part from trade agreement concessions) have been the major factor causing or threatening to cause the serious injury (or, in the case of workers, the unemployment or underemployment).

That is, the petitioner must now sustain the double burden of proving both that the increased imports were caused in major part by trade concessions and that the increased imports were the major factor in causing the serious injury. In this way, a preponderant dual causal link between trade concessions and increased imports and between increased imports and serious injury must be established. In so doing, the Commission appears to have made these tests an almost impossible burden of proof [46, p. 1334].[9]

As in the application of the second criterion, the Commission has not been successful in producing convincing evidence of cause-and-effect linkages between increased imports and injury, nor indeed, between any other condition of trade and injury. This should not be too surprising, since many of these injury-causing factors are not quantifiable and cannot be subjected to appropriate statistical treatment.

In summary, then, it would appear that determining the eligibility of an industry, firm, or group of workers for adjustment assistance under the foregoing criteria has been rather difficult, mostly because of the required double show of causality and because of the paucity of supporting data that could be fitted into a statistical model that could materially assist the decision process.

A number of proposals have been advanced in and out of the Congress to revise adjustment assistance. Some have been directed at overcoming problems related to the implementation of the program, while others urge a fundamentally different approach to the whole problem.

Reflecting the consensus of the times, President Richard Nixon,

---

[8] Most cases investigated by the Commission have resulted in findings of injury or the lack of it, while few cases have found threatened injury where none existed before. In one such case, it was observed that even though the piano industry was not at the time seriously injured by imports, an anticipated increase in imports due to tariff reductions could cause serious injury [86].

[9] If the Commission rules in the affirmative, the Secretary of Labor (Commerce) may proceed to certify the workers (firms) eligible to apply for adjustment assistance. In cases where a tie occurs, the President of the United States decides eligibility.

in his proposed Trade Act of 1969, called for a relaxation of the TEA criteria. The proposal would have required that the injury-causing increased imports should not be causally linked to prior trade agreement concessions. Further, such imports would not be required to be the major cause of serious injury, but only a substantial cause, with obviously different implications. Under the changes suggested in this proposal and in several variants of it [93], adjustment assistance could be provided to industries, firms, or workers regardless of the cause of increased imports.

The proposed Trade Act of 1969 was never acted upon by the Congress and was supplanted with newer, more sweeping trade legislation. The latter was introduced to the House Committee on Ways and Means on April 10, 1973 under the title of the Trade Reform Bill [94]; it remained in Congress for 20 months, and finally emerged as the Trade Act of 1974, which President Gerald Ford signed into law on January 3, 1975.

Significant changes are evident in this new trade legislation. Perhaps the most important change is the elimination of the strict causal linkages that were at the heart of the TEA. Domestic industries, firms, or workers now have to show only that imports are a substantial cause of injury rather than the major cause—the former term meaning a cause that is important and not less than any other cause [91, p. 35]. Likewise, in the provisions for adjustment assistance to workers [91, p. 42] and firms [91, p. 53], the term "contributed importantly" is used and defined as a "cause which is important but not necessarily more important than any other cause" [91, p. 53]. Under earlier legislation, it was imperative to attempt the identification of government-induced injury, since the justification for adjustment assistance is compensation for a government action. Under current legislation, there is the implicit danger that adjustment assistance may degenerate into a general subsidy scheme and become a form of social insurance for inefficiency or misfortune only remotely connected with import impact. The difficult problem of determining causality between increased imports and trade concessions is greatly softened in the new legislation but, in the process, the logical basis of the program is severely compromised—if not destroyed [45, p. 78]. These changes, as Bale consistently maintains, represent a shift in philosophical orientation away from specialized adjustment assistance to a generalized program based on expediency considerations [45, p. 79].

Other important provisions of the Trade Act of 1974 may be

briefly mentioned. Tariffs on numerous products manufactured in the less-developed countries would be eliminated to give them preference over goods from industrial countries. Relief from competition of cheap imports under existing antidumping and countervailing duty laws is relaxed and made somewhat easier to obtain, and the entire procedure is greatly accelerated. Adjustment assistance to workers has been somewhat increased. Trade Readjustment Allowance (TRA) benefits would now be 70% of the worker's average weekly wages, compared to 65% under the TEA. Duration of said benefits is retained at the same level as in the earlier legislation, namely 52 weeks with the usual extensions of 26 weeks for workers in training programs and/or older workers. Relocation allowance, training, and job-search benefits remain virtually unchanged [95, Titles V and III, pp. 42–47].

Conspicuously absent from the legislation is a proposal advanced in 1972 by the National Association of Manufacturers (NAM), which commanded some congressional support. This proposal would have provided for the establishment of an early warning, or forecasting, system that would give firms advance notice of impending injury, thereby allowing early delivery of government aid to avert dislocation and unemployment before they occurred [34]. Early warning, although an untested concept, would channel applicant firms into the adjustment process earlier than under current legislation. It would provide a shift in emphasis from present injury compensation to preinjury adjustment and self-help.

In conclusion, it would seem that while the basic thrust of the new trade legislation is in the liberal direction, the future outline and implementation of adjustment assistance remains unclear.

2.   THE RATIONALE OF ADJUSTMENT ASSISTANCE

To date a rigorous theory of adjustment assistance is lacking. All that can be done, as Bale suggests [45, p. 49], is to frame the basic issues and implications in general terms. While tariff concessions may produce desirable results for the economy as a whole, they may produce adverse effects on a number of domestic industries particularly affected by changes in trade policy. When dislocation occurs, the government must assume the responsibility to minimize the resulting market distortions and should absorb, at least in part, the cost of readjustment to alternate lines of activity.

Clearly, the rationale and basic assumptions governing adjustment assistance are important and raise a number of fundamental questions that require consideration. Is there a need for trade adjustment assistance? What is the role of such assistance within the context of changing foreign economic policy? How can assistance be justified for firms and workers affected by import competition, while similar assistance is denied when injury comes as a result of other economic forces? Is adjustment assistance an indication that something is fundamentally wrong with market forces? Can dislocation caused by import competition be isolated from other contributing factors? It is to a partial examination of these questions that we turn presently.

Admittedly, foreign trade plays a relatively minor role in the overall GNP of the United States (about 5%), and import dislocation typically accounts for only a fraction of the total economic adjustment problems on a national scale. Of much larger significance are the major structural shifts induced by changes in technology, consumer taste and preferences, and, more recently, changes in defense and environmental activities. It is estimated, for example, that changes in military spending affected 2 million jobs in the 1968–1971 period alone, whereas changes due to import competition seldom affect more than 200,000 jobs annually [35, pp. 20–22]. On the surface, many critics would not see a need or justification for a major program of adjustment assistance. On the other hand, the severity of import competition may now be a relatively greater factor in economic dislocation than in previous years, and may require substantial shifts of resources into alternate economic endeavors. Adjustment assistance may, therefore, be viewed as a prerequisite to foster the orderly transfer of resources by subsidizing those factors—usually labor—that actually move [3, p. 112]. Insofar as the alternative to adjustment assistance is direct protection, the former is preferable, since it protects or at least supplements real incomes without embalming or protecting existing production patterns that may well be inefficient [3, p. 111]. In this way, adjustment assistance is needed in order that injury to firms and workers caused by import competition would be corrected on a domestic rather than international level [24]. That is, individual adjustment assistance is exclusively tailored to the need of firms that are in difficulty and of workers who have lost their jobs. Helping them would, of course, entail some cost to the taxpayer on the justification that these firms and workers are the victims of the national policy of trade liberalization. The benefits of that policy to consumers (taxpayers) and to the economy would normally be greater than the costs incurred for adjustment assistance, as our estimates of cost and benefit have shown.

Certainly, government intervention is needed and justified when there is evidence of conspicuous "neighborhood effects," and private decisions may be insufficient to realize a maximization of social welfare [45, p. 191].

It may be argued—on equity considerations—that there is no valid reason why workers and firms displaced by import competition should receive special compensation that those displaced for different economic reasons do not receive. The failure of conventional macro policy to sustain full employment and to ease the reabsorption of displaced resources has dramatically brought home the fact that import impact is only one of many possible causes of economic dislocation and unemployment. To compensate injury due to import competition without commensurate compensation for other government-induced injury is discriminatory and inequitable [45, p. 194].

Adjustment assistance does not imply that there is something basically wrong with market forces. It is, rather, an acceptance of the reality of international competition which, at times, prevents free market directives from operating efficiently everywhere. Import impact, for example, coincided with the virtual doubling of United States imports in the 1960s. This development, coupled with domestic inflation, has had unfortunate repercussions on the competitive posture of the United States in world markets. Admittedly, American wage rates have been higher than in the rest of the world but, historically, they have been offset by the higher productivity of American labor, as evidenced by consistent surpluses on current account in the Balance of Payments. This positive trade balance peaked in the early 1960s, dropped to $3.7 billion, and in 1971 showed a deficit for the first time [24, pp. 824–826]. Thus, lagging productivity and domestic inflation have weakened United States competitiveness in world markets in some traditional lines of manufacturing.

It is clear, then, that the logic of trade adjustment assistance rests in part on the realities of changing patterns of competition in international trade and the related obligation of government to ease the resulting economic dislocation. The process of adjustment may not work perfectly, since it is often difficult to determine precisely the relationship between import penetration and the scores of other factors causing dislocation.

At times, society may provide public funds for political, as distinct from economic, reasons. A generous worker adjustment assistance program may go a long way in winning the support of organized labor for a particular platform such as free trade [45, p. 192]. In the last decade, however, organized labor has moved steadily away from its earlier tradition of free trade toward a more protectionist posture favoring the adoption of massive trade restrictions. The Burke-Hartke Bill, which won strong labor support, would have (if acted upon) put virtually all United States imports under quotas, exluding only those commodities not produced at all domestically [14].[10] This heightened dissatisfaction on the part of labor is not entirely unjustified. At best, only about 50,000 workers have been certified to apply for adjustment assistance [16, Table 3] as of the end of 1974. The benefits received have been almost totally in the form of TRA compensation. Negligible retraining benefits have been provided, fewer job placement services have been offered and/or accepted, and practically no relocation allowances have been paid. The net result is that the displaced worker is in very much the same position as without the adjustment program.

After all is said and done, it should be remembered that, under all the programs, statistics, and bureaucracy, is the individual worker who faces the trauma of job loss and the unknowns of unemployment. The heavy emphasis on TRA payments—often as a retroactive lump-sum payment—has tended to neglect the other positive aspects of adjustment assistance that might enhance the worker's chances to regain employment quickly with good job retention. Indeed, the concepts of retraining, job search, and relocation, which are part of the whole package of adjustment assistance, are basically good and could be made viable given favorable conditions. The resulting benefits to both the worker and society of a real adjustment program could be very substantial. The worker could quickly regain productive employment, often in a better position, with renewed income and pride. Society would also gain by removing the unemployed worker from the public rolls and add him to the producing side of the ledger, thus benefiting from both decreased transfer payments and increased production and tax revenue [34, p. 49].

Existing legislation as it has evolved from the TEA of 1962 does not seem, on the whole, to provide for rational trade adjustment

[10] See also newspaper articles that reflect the sentiment of organized labor [62] and others, too numerous to list.

assistance. If meaningful reform is not forthcoming—even beyond the Trade Act of 1974—the alternatives are either an increase in demand for more trade restrictions on the part of organized labor and business firms, or a continuation of the current practice of limited, sporadic, and inefficient compensation to firms and workers injured by import competition.

3. ADJUSTMENT EXPERIENCE IN FOOTWEAR

In general terms, adjustment experience has produced mixed results. Between 1962 and 1974, the Commission issued determinations on 249 petitions covering some 110,200 workers [16, p. 2]. However, from 1962 to almost the end of 1969, no petitions for tariff adjustment or for assistance to firms and workers were granted. Finally, in November 1969, the Commission for the first time, granted three worker petitions for adjustment assistance, which coincided with the application of the more liberal "but for" test detailed in the first section of this chapter [16, p. 2]. In the wake of these determinations, the Commission produced a flurry of affirmative findings based largely on interpretative rather than substantive changes in the law.

The specific experience of the footwear industry is detailed in Table IV-1, which indicates that between 1962 and 1974, total footwear petitions amounted to 118, covering a total of 30,609 workers. On a relative basis, footwear petitions represent 47% (nearly half) of total petitions, while petitioning footwear workers represent about 28% of all petitioning workers. This suggests that footwear appears to be more seriously import impacted relative to other industries. Indeed, nearly three-quarters of the determinations issued during this period, originated in three industrial groups: nonrubber footwear, electrical equipment, and textiles, with 118, 44, and 24 petitions, respectively [16, p. 2].

Actual TRA expenditure amounted to $72,787,498 as of December 31, 1974, and out of this total, $18,706,387 (25.7%) was allocated specifically to the footwear industry, with all the allocation experienced between 1970 and 1974.[11]

A further breakdown of the data reveals that of the 118 footwear

---

[11] Information graciously furnished by G. Barlow, International Labor Affairs Bureau (ILAB), in a telephone conversation, April 29, 1975.

TABLE IV-1

Petition Experience in Footwear, 1962–1974

	Petitions denied	Workers denied	Petitions approved	Workers approved	Petitions
Men's shoes	16	4320	1	230	17
Women's shoes[a]	59	13,102	42	12,957	101
Workers	75	17,422	43	13,187	118 (petitions) 30,609 (workers)

[a] Of the fifty-nine women's shoes petitions denied, one produced girls' shoes; one produced tennis shoes; one produced slippers; and two produced both men's and women's shoes. All others produced women's shoes exclusively or predominantly.

SOURCE: Compiled from *Trade Adjustment Assistance Calendar*, prepared by the United States Department of Labor, International Labor Affairs Bureau, Office of Foreign Economic Policy.

petitions, 75 of them involving an estimated 17,422 workers were denied, while 43 with an estimated 13,187 workers were certified. Looking at each group of shoes separately, in the women's category, 42 petitions covering some 12,957 workers were approved, while 59 petitions with 13,102 workers were denied. Stated somewhat differently, approved petitions in women's footwear amounted to 98% of total approved petitions, while denied petitions in the same group represent 79% of total denied footwear petitions. In the men's footwear group, all but 1 petition involving 230 workers were denied. Total denied petitions in this group amounted to 16, covering an estimated 4320 workers. The foregoing data would seem to imply that the certifying agencies have consistently viewed the women's footwear group to be more seriously import impacted than the corresponding men's group, or footwear in general.

Statistical tests of independence between types of shoes produced and approved/denied petitions, on the one hand, and between types of shoes produced and associated workers, on the other, are detailed in contingency tables (a) and (b) of Table IV-2. Actual frequencies are recorded in each cell, accompanied by the corresponding theoretical frequencies shown in parentheses. Computed chi-square values (χ_0^2) are shown at the foot of each table along with the expected chi-square values (χ_ϵ^2) at the conventional levels. The results of these tests, which are highly significant, clearly indicate that it is easier for

TABLE IV-2

Chi-Square Tests of Independence

Group	Petitions			Petitions		
	Denied	Approved	Total	Denied	Approved	Total
	(a)			**(b)**		
Men's	16 (11)	1 (6)	17	4320 (2590)	230 (1960)	4550
Women's	59 (64)	42 (37)	101	13,102 (14,832)	12,957 (11,227)	26,059
Total	75	43	118	17,422	13,187	30,609
	$\chi_0^2 = 7.51$, $\chi_\epsilon^2 = 3.8$			$\chi_0^2 = 3150.9$, $\chi_\epsilon^2 = 3.8$		
	6.6			6.6		

Region	**(c)**			**(d)**		
New England	34 (42)	32 (24)	66	9425 (11,040)	10,171 (8556)	19,596
Mid-Atlantic	19 (16)	7 (10)	26	3006 (2773)	1915 (2148)	4921
North-Central	12 (9)	2 (5)	14	3048 (2038)	570 (1580)	3618
South and West	9 (7)	2 (4)	11	1538 (1166)	531 (903)	2069
Total	74	43	117	17,017	13,187	30,204
	$\chi_0^2 = 10.02$, $\chi_\epsilon^2 = 7.7$, d.f. $= 3$			$\chi_0^2 = 2004.2$, $\chi_\epsilon^2 = 7.7$, d.f. $= 3$		
	11.3			11.3		

SOURCE: Tables IV-1 and IV-3.

workers/firms engaged in the production of women's shoes to get approval of petitions, followed by adjustment assistance, than for the other groups. Moreover, this apparent bias in favor of women's shoes seems to be compounded by a further regional bias in the award of petitions for adjustment assistance. In contingency tables (c) and (d), we have tabulated the regional distribution of leather products petitions (almost totally footwear) for the period October 1962–February 1975. Data utilized were extracted and aggregated from Table IV-3, which details the state distribution of leather products petitions, excluding Puerto Rico.

Once again, the results are statistically significant, lending support to the regional bias hypothesis postulated above. At this time we can only speculate as to the reasons why such biases exist. It would seem that firms/workers qualifying for adjustment assistance may lag both in technological innovation and in the ready adaptation to chang-

TABLE IV-3

State Distribution of Leather Products Petitions,
October 1962–February 1975

State	Certified petitions	Workers certified	Denied petitions	Workers denied
Arkansas	—	—	1	200
California	1	100	3	378
Connecticut	—	—	3	287
Florida	1	431	3	275
Georgia	—	—	2	685
Illinois	2	570	—	—
Indiana	—	—	1	300
Maine	3	910	9	3869
Massachusetts	18	5849	19	4239
Missouri	—	—	8	2255
New Hampshire	11	3412	2	295
New Jersey	1	90	1	65
New York	5	1660	12	1593
Ohio	—	—	3	493
Pennsylvania	1	165	6	1348
Puerto Rico	—	—	4	920
Vermont	—	—	1	735
Total	43	13,187	78	17,937

SOURCE: G. Barlow, International Labor Affairs Bureau (ILAB), United States Department of Labor.

ing market conditions. Typically, applicants of this type are small, closely held companies, often managed by a single family, with a work force that may be old and not highly productive. Probably, this unwillingness or inability to adapt to changing conditions contributes to the firms' failure to adjust effectively to the impact of import competition. Harold Bratt, for example, reports that in adjustment proposals certified for three footwear firms, allocations were made for working capital, technical assistance, and new machinery and equipment. One of the proposals actually provided for investment in new equipment that represented a significant innovation for this firm, namely, string lasting and injection molding. Yet, even in the presence of such a favorable innovative climate, this firm as well as the other two firms, continued to produce the same cheap line of women's shoes as they had done all along prior to the adjustment [49, pp. 21–22].

Alternately, as brought out in Chapter I, the certifying agencies may well be aware of the high degree of specialization characteristic of the industry and of its attendant implications. That is, many of the smaller firms tend to specialize in the production of a limited range of footwear, and this specialization may relate to men's, women's, or children's shoes; to expensive, medium-priced, or cheap shoes; to general-purpose or casual shoes; and to different methods of fabrication, all of which tend to limit severely the typical production run. Rapid changes in style and fashion tend to compound these problems—particularly in women's footwear—all in all making for a precarious existence. Thus, in a Commission report, the dissenting opinion stated that "despite the company's adoption of the latest styles in response to changing fashions, the (company) has been unable to sell its footwear profitably in competition with increasing imports" [87]. It would seem, therefore, that the major fashion centers in Europe—notably Italy and Spain—are in a more favorable position to exploit the rising demand for stylish, comfortable, high-quality women's footwear than their domestic counterparts.

Moreover, the industry landscape shows up important regional and area differences in plant size and price lines. In Massachusetts, for example, the typical plant size is smaller, on the average, than in Missouri. Within New England, plants in Maine and New Hampshire tend to be substantially larger than those in Massachusetts. Important differences also prevail in plant size according to type of shoes produced. Producers of men's shoes tend to operate larger plants, while producers of women's shoes operate medium-sized and small plants. Production of women's shoes is predominant in New England; Pennsylvania produces a large number of misses' and children's shoes; while Wisconsin is mostly a men's shoe production center. The South and West tend to specialize in the higher-priced shoes and New England in the low- and medium-priced lines.[12] All these factors lend some support and justification to the apparent regional bias and bias in favor of women's shoes in the award of adjustment petitions.

Finally, it may well be that the political process works to the particular advantage of certain regions and/or types of footwear. In the final stage of deliberations leading to the passage of the Trade Act of 1974, Senator Thomas J. McIntyre (Democrat, New Hampshire) proposed a rather restrictive amendment to the legislation, aimed at the protection of domestic footwear and detailing the plight of certain

---

[12] Impressions gained by the authors upon visiting a number of footwear establishments in the New England and Mid-Atlantic regions.

communities that seemed to be particularly import impacted. The amendment was subsequently rejected by the Senate in a 49/35 vote, with opponents arguing, in effect, that other provisions of the legislation together with forthcoming international negotiations would be more effective in relieving the problems of the industry [61].

In the last 5 or 6 years, there have been a number of studies dealing with the problems of import penetration and adjustment assistance in the footwear industry. Some of these were undertaken by government agencies, while others have come from independent scholars and researchers. Some have official government sanction, while others may be used as internal sources of information only. In this last section, we propose to review, however briefly, some of the more significant findings.

The Task Force [38][13] study on nonrubber footwear (1969), which was largely descriptive in nature, found no competitive injury to the industry as a whole. It concluded that most footwear imports supplemented rather than supplanted domestic production, and that imports have actually opened up a new alternative to domestic consumers. Allowing for some substitution between domestic and imported shoes, the team found that the import share competing directly with domestic production ranges between 10 to 15% in pairage terms and much less in value terms. While it recognized some impact in the women's and misses' market, it still believes that imported leather footwear is a relatively small share in this market—the great bulk of imported footwear being made up mostly of low-priced slippers, sandals, and vinyl shoes. The men's and boys' market and the children's market show a much smaller import penetration in both absolute and relative terms and do not appear to be import impacted [38, p. 3].

The Task Force, then, looked upon the problems experienced by the industry as being rather sporadic in nature and confined to certain communities or regions. On a national scale, it viewed the problem of import penetration as a rather minor one in terms of adverse impact on the entire industry, its employment, or upon the national welfare [38, p. 4]. However, in its recommendations, the Task Force hastened to point out that the specific areas, firms, and workers who have been seriously injured by import competition do require attention and assistance.

---

[13] The Task Force included representatives from the Departments of Commerce, Labor, Treasury, and State under the direction of the Special Representative for Trade Negotiations.

Adjustment assistance, however, like any other scarce resource, ought to be rationally and efficiently allocated even for localized areas that visibly experience import injury. The Task Force reports, for example, that local unemployment offices experienced a negligible impact from plant closings, due to either the small size of the firm involved in relation to the area's total labor force, or to the fact that alternate employment was readily available in other local shoe plants or in other industries. A few areas actually reported a shortage of skilled shoe workers [38, p. 75]. Undoubtedly, Massachusetts has been characterized as an import-impacted community—an area where segments of the shoe industry have historically been concentrated. During 1969–1972, for example, nine Haverhill shoe factories employing some 1559 workers closed down. Yet, an exploratory trip by NAM to various areas of the New England shoe industry in 1972 [34, 25] revealed much activity in certain specialty lines. Bucking the general tide in the industry, these firms were advertising and pleading with the local unemployment offices to supply them with skilled shoe workers. While employment in the industry generally was declining, these firms were still hiring [34, p. 66].

In 1970 President Richard Nixon gave priority attention to the problem of market penetration by imported nonrubber footwear and instructed the then Tariff Commission to investigate the problems facing the industry. In its final report [97], the Commission made no findings, since four commissioners divided equally. Disagreement centered on the causal relation between rising imports and concessions granted under trade agreements. Two commissioners ruled that the increased imports were not caused in major part by the trade concessions. After separating the industry into several major components, it reached a qualified conclusion that some competitive pressure was being felt in some segments of the industry such as women's dress/casual and men's dress/casual shoes, and that the smaller producers (typically the most vulnerable) sustained the hardest impact. The Commission viewed some of these trends as accelerating and intensifying in the future if some relief were not provided, and to that end, it recommended modest tariff increases on a few key categories of imported footwear, coupled with an adjustment assistance program for firms and workers that were seriously injured by import competition.

On the specific problem of trade adjustment assistance, the pioneering work was undertaken in February 1972 by the International

Labor Affairs Bureau (ILAB) of the United States Department of Labor [16]. Four groups of shoe workers (experimental group) and eight groups of workers separated from nonshoe companies (control group), totaling 424 workers, were surveyed in 12 states of the East, South, and Midwest. The purpose of the study was to determine the experience and present condition of workers allegedly displaced because of import competition. It may be added parenthetically that even though the survey was carried out in a swift and hurried manner (in 2 months) and is therefore subject to weaknesses and criticisms, the time dimension was clearly more appropriate than it would be in 1975, a year in which a multitude of causes produced rampant unemployment. In other words, the ILAB team was probably more successful in separating out import-impacted unemployment from unemployment in general, than a similar contemporary survey ever could.

Some of the important findings that emerged from the survey are detailed in Table IV-4. By way of comparison between the two groups, it is evident that shoe workers had shorter service in import-impacted employment; that they earned on the average somewhat less; that a smaller proportion of them were receiving TRA benefits; and that they fared somewhat better in terms of job placement and retraining in relation to the nonshoe control group.

The above findings seem to suggest that shoe workers' investment in time on the job is less than in the control group; that the ability to absorb displaced workers is somewhat greater in the footwear industry, where skills are more easily transferable; and that footwear workers are, perhaps, not as seriously import impacted as workers in the control group.

Significantly, however, the much longer time lag between separation from trade-impacted employment and the receipt of adjustment assistance in footwear makes it dramatically clear that the cost of readjustment to the displaced worker and to society is greater, the longer the average duration of unemployment. Hence, this time lag should be substantially reduced. On the average, TRA payments reach the displaced worker almost a year after the date of unemployment, and, as such, this form of assistance has been aptly described as "burial expenses" [34, p. 8]. By the time the worker receives the benefits, his 52 weeks eligibility period for retraining and other assistance has usually expired. The result is a lump-sum retroactive payment to the worker without the opportunity to benefit from the other

TABLE IV-4

Adjustment Experience of Shoe and Nonshoe Workers, 1972

Tested characteristic	Shoe workers	Nonshoe workers
1. Length of service in import-impacted employment	6.7 years	10.4 years
2. Average hourly wage	$2.41	$2.86
3. Proportion of workers absorbed in same industry	52%	40%
4. Proportion of workers involuntarily laid off	79%	89%
5. Proportion of workers employed since separation from import-impacted employment	57%	46%
6. Average unemployment benefits received	$46 per week	$57 per week
7. Proportion of workers receiving TRA benefits	13%	21%
8. Average TRA eligibility consumed	38 weeks	27 weeks
9. Time lags (between separation from impacted firm and TRA certification)	45 weeks	26 weeks

SOURCE: International Labor Affairs Bureau, "Survey of Workers Displaced by Import Competition" (internal study), United States Department of Labor, Washington D.C., 1972.

aspects of the package designed to facilitate reemployment and/or relocation. In this way, the real potential benefits of a viable assistance program are only seldom implemented and realized.

The retraining concept, in particular, is probably of greater significance in long-run adjustment than any amount of retroactive TRA payments. Usually, the skills of displaced workers acquired over many years are downgraded, since the import-affected firms where these workers are employed are viewed as part of a "sick" industry whose skills will die with it. The interests of society would be far better served if top priority were given to presently possessed skills in the reemployment process. A classic example of the potential benefits of retraining, cited in the NAM exploratory trip, is a Rhode Island shoe factory that laid off several hundred workers, 287 of which entered a training program. As of the end of 1972, 207 workers (or 72%) completed their training course, with 172 (or 60%) successfully reabsorbed into the active labor force as a direct result of such training [34, p. 25].

Perhaps the least recognized potential benefit of adjustment assistance is the provision for relocation allowance. This is available only to heads of households, and it would pay for the moving costs of the worker, his family, and their household items, plus a lump-sum payment of 2.5 times the national average weekly manufacturing wage [90, p. 47].[14] Almost no use has been made of this type of assistance. The reasons for this inactivity are obvious. Older workers, in particular, display considerable inertia and resistance to moving. Then, too, it must be recognized that, in addition to the actual cost of physically moving from one location to another, there is the "psychic" cost that must be factored in. Unquestionably, even in a highly mobile society like ours, the severance of community ties, moving children between schools, leaving close friends and relationships, etc., exact a psychic fee [22, p. 72]. It is also true, however, that partially offsetting the psychic cost, may be a renewed sense of self-confidence, a steady income, and being off the unemployment lines.

The ILAB data were subjected to further statistical treatment by McCarthy [31] and Bale [45]; the latter is more general in scope and the former is localized to the Massachusetts shoe industry. Since prolific use of regression analysis was made in both studies, there was no explicit need for control groups, since the technique isolates the effects of each variable individually, while keeping other variables constant, or in control.

Bale develops two variants of a model to estimate the costs to a displaced worker and to society of adjusting to import competition. With specific reference to the footwear industry, his findings indicate that import-impacted shoe workers remain unemployed for 38 weeks on the average. Their average weekly wage—estimated via regression—is $102, making the total foregone wages for the duration of unemployment $3876 ($102 × 38). While unemployed, displaced shoe workers received transfer payments (unemployment benefits and TRA) averaging $1625, leaving a net loss in lost wages of $2251 ($3876—$1625). If the displaced shoe worker reenters the active labor force, his average hourly wage tends to be smaller by about 3¢ than in the previous job, $2.81 per hour. If this wage differential is made up in 1 year, his total loss will be $2307 ($2251 + $56); while if he never makes

---

[14] Similar provisions held under TEA of 1962.

up the difference, the discounted value of his lost wages up to retirement age must be added to the stream of lost wages, making for a total
loss of $2890 ($2251 + $639). The cost to society generated by each
unemployed shoe worker will equal the worker's new wage rate ($2.81)
multiplied by the average work week (36 hr), multiplied further by the
average duration of unemployment (38 weeks), or an estimated $3844
[45, pp. 180–181]. At $3844 per worker, the cost to society of these
displaced import-impacted shoe workers will be $53.8 million[15] ($3844
× 13,000) if we apply the foregoing estimates to the roughly 13,000
displaced workers in footwear covered by the forty-three approved
petitions as of the end of 1974 (see Table IV-1).

The collective cost to workers themselves would range between
$32.3 million ($2307 × 13,000) and $40.5 million ($2890 × 13,000),
which implies that a substantial part of the total adjustment cost must
be borne by the displaced workers, collectively and individually.

Our own estimates of the costs and benefits of trade liberalization
(conservative as they are) indicate that the gains to society as a whole
will more than compensate for any loss incurred by the affected group.
This suggests that adjustment assistance to the injured workers/firms
out of the general tax revenue would be amply justified on economic
grounds.

[15] Bale's estimates turn out to be much larger than those indicated here, since he
assumes a decrease in employment in the footwear industry of 25,000 workers. Actually,
unemployment data in footwear is not available. The closest relevant measure is United
States Department of Labor data on the number of insured unemployed whose last
employment was in establishments producing leather and leather products of which
two-thirds is estimated to be in footwear. In effect, we make the implicit assumption that
only certified workers are actually displaced by import competition, although, realistically, some of the workers whose petitions for adjustment assistance have been denied
may also be seriously injured by import competition.

REGRESSION ANALYSIS

GLOSSARY OF TERMS[1]

W/M	womens' and misses' footwear
M/B	men's and boys' footwear
C/I	children's and infants' footwear
T	total footwear
Wk	work shoes
Ath	athletic shoes
Slp	slippers
Oth	other footwear (predominantly vinyl, not classified by sex)
Q_m	import quantity (million pairs) according to seven digit TSUSA
q_m	import quantity (per capita pairs)
$\bar{Q}_m$	value of imports deflated by import unit-value index
$\bar{q}_m$	$\bar{Q}_m$/relevant population
Q_d	domestic production − exports (million pairs)
q_d	domestic production − exports (per capita pairs)
$\bar{Q}_d$	value of domestic production deflated by relevant domestic price index
$\bar{q}_d$	$\bar{Q}_d$/relevant population
Q_c	import quantity + domestic quantity (million pairs)
q_c	Q_c/relevant population
P_{M_2}	weighted import unit-value index
P_W	general WPI and WPI for total footwear and component groups
P_{M_1}	simple import unit-value index
p_{m_2}	P_{M_2}/general domestic WPI
p_{m_1}	P_{M_1}/general domestic WPI
P_D	relevant domestic footwear WPI
p_d	relevant domestic footwear WPI/general WPI
p_m/p_d	ratio of import to domestic footwear price
P_C	composite price index (import + domestic)
p_c	P_C/general WPI
y	real disposable per capita income
T	trend
p_ℓ	leather WPI/general WPI
c_u	capacity utilization rate
p_{hs}	hides and skins WPI/general WPI
w	wage rate of footwear production workers/general WPI
k	capital expenditure per production worker (nonrubber)/general WPI
k_n	expenditure on new machinery and equipment per production worker/general WPI
p_a	outer apparel WPI (excluding footwear)/general WPI
pce	personal consumption expenditure per capita in 1958 dollars
V_M	nominal value of footwear imports (thousand dollars)
v_m	V_M/relevant population group
Y	nominal disposable personal income
Y^*	Y/total population
V_d	nominal value of domestic footwear production
P_L	WPI for leather not deflated by general WPI
W	nominal wage rate of footwear production workers
Y_r	real disposable personal income
p_{m_4}	Italian footwear price index
p_{m_4}/p_d	ratio of Italian footwear price/domestic footwear price

[1]Capital letter variables indicate undeflated series; lowercase variables indicate deflated series.

131

DATA SHEET

Year	Q_m(M/B)	Q_m(W/M)	Q_m(C/I)	Q_m(Wk)	Q_m(Ath)	Q_m(Slp)
1955						
1956						
1957						
1958						
1959						
1960	5.2	7.7	0.1			
1961	5.4	9.6	0.2			
1962	7.5	13.5	0.9			
1963	7.7	18.2	0.8			
1964	13.9	47.9	2.3	0.2	0.4	2.3
1965	16.3	52.0	3.6	0.8	1.1	8.4
1966	16.9	62.9	6.0	1.1	1.2	2.6
1967	21.0	90.0	7.5	1.5	1.4	1.6
1968	28.9	125.5	9.3	1.6	1.8	2.0
1969	35.0	130.3	13.3	1.9	2.5	2.1
1970	45.1	153.3	15.1	1.8	4.3	1.9
1971	53.2	168.3	15.8	2.0	5.5	1.8
1972	55.2	180.8	20.3	2.4	6.2	1.7
1973	53.6	186.1	16.8	3.2	6.3	1.6
1974	75.6	189.4	19.0			
1975	84.7	198.6	18.0			

Year	q_m(T)	Q_m(M/B)	$\tilde{Q}_m$(W/M)	$\tilde{Q}_m$(C/I)	Q_m(Slp)	$\tilde{Q}_m$(Wk)
1955						
1956						
1957						
1958						
1959						
1960						
1961						
1962						
1963						
1964	0.3659	35.3	59.0	1.3	1.6	0.4
1965	0.4679	38.2	64.7	2.6	2.3	3.1
1966	0.4998	48.4	66.7	4.8	1.9	3.7
1967	0.6567	61.8	122.8	6.2	1.5	5.1
1968	0.8939	89.3	189.4	6.7	1.7	5.7
1969	0.9694	116.7	188.9	10.5	1.6	6.9
1970	1.1369	136.3	235.3	12.5	1.5	6.9
1971	1.2531	162.9	280.3	13.6	1.3	7.9
1972	1.3454	173.6	328.1	18.4	1.1	9.5
1973	1.3599	176.8	354.5	15.7	1.3	13.3
1974			258.9	15.8		
1975			271.7	14.9		

Q_m(Oth)	q_m(M/B)	q_m(W/M)	q_m(C/I)	q_m(Wk)	Q_m(Ath)[a]	q_m(Slp)[b]
2.4	0.1873	0.6173	0.0565	0.0015	0.0021	0.0130
7.6	0.2156	0.6576	0.0889	0.0114	0.0057	0.0431
6.2	0.2216	0.7815	0.1512	0.0134	0.0060	0.0132
5.4	0.2706	1.0981	0.1899	0.0185	0.0072	0.0079
7.4	0.3359	1.5030	0.2407	0.0196	0.0090	0.0100
8.0	0.4369	1.5290	0.3554	0.0241	0.0124	0.0104
8.0	0.5537	1.7733	0.4072	0.0217	0.0209	0.0094
9.4	0.6438	1.9150	0.4321	0.0237	0.0268	0.0089
11.2	0.6580	2.0260	0.5657	0.0280	0.0301	0.0084
15.7	0.6307	2.0544	0.4802	0.0373	0.0299	0.0074

$\bar{Q}_m$(Ath)	$\bar{Q}_m$(T)	$\bar{Q}_m$(Oth)	$\bar{Q}_m$(M/B)	$\bar{Q}_m$(W/M/C/I)	$\tilde{q}_m$(M/B)	$\tilde{q}_m$(W/M)
	7.3					
	8.9					
	11.4					
	31.0					
	23.3					
	40.3		15.4	19.5		
	32.8		16.3	12.7		
	50.1		21.4	18.6		
	70.8		25.4	33.6		
4.3	116.3	5.3	40.8	66.2	0.4777	0.7610
11.7	150.5	6.6	47.7	73.5	0.5076	0.8201
12.1	162.7	3.4	50.1	90.8	0.6341	0.8290
13.8	215.6	4.3	61.8	129.2	0.7958	1.4992
17.6	212.7	7.2	84.9	178.2	1.1315	2.2691
22.1	324.7	9.1	102.9	189.1	1.4562	2.2172
28.4	385.6	12.0	132.6	222.2	1.6748	2.7214
39.4	430.4	14.4	156.6	243.5	1.9716	3.1886
47.4	466.9	16.3	162.3	265.6	2.0695	3.6758
57.3	474.0	19.5	157.7	267.9	2.0787	3.9147
	493.9		222.6	274.7	2.5823	2.8203
	538.1		249.7	286.6	2.8603	2.9152

[a] Total pairs/male adult population.
[b] Total pairs/total population.

Year	$\tilde{q}_m$(C/I)	$\tilde{q}_m$(Slp)	$\tilde{q}_m$(Wk)	$\tilde{q}_m$(W/M/C/I)	$\tilde{q}_m$(M/B)	$\tilde{q}_m$(W/M/C/I)
1955						
1956						
1957						
1958						
1959						
1960					0.2254	0.1797
1961					0.2330	0.1146
1962					0.3022	0.1653
1963					0.3536	0.2943
1964	0.0303	0.0206	0.0098	0.5489	0.5512	0.5614
1965	0.0649	0.0292	0.0733	0.5648	0.6350	0.6169
1966	0.1212	0.0236	0.0835	0.7615	0.6515	0.7555
1967	0.1579	0.0183	0.1128	1.0660	0.7958	1.0673
1968	0.1762	0.0204	0.1226	1.3968	1.0759	1.4831
1969	0.2805	0.0188	0.1432	1.6279	1.2846	1.5430
1970	0.3363	0.0174	0.1432	2.0058	1.6292	1.7992
1971	0.3732	0.0148	0.1639	2.2488	1.8943	1.9577
1972	0.5156	0.0123	0.1900	2.7727	1.9352	2.1251
1973	0.4503	0.0143	0.2543	2.9514	1.8549	2.1366
1974	0.4661				2.5832	2.1849
1975	0.4488				2.8608	2.2683

Year	Q_d(Oth)	$\tilde{Q}_d$(M/B)	$\tilde{Q}_d$(W/M/C/I)	$\tilde{Q}_d$(T) = Q_s(T)	q_d(M/B)	q_d(W/M)
1955				2659.9		
1956				2675.9		
1957				2671.7		
1958				2629.2		
1959				2749.8		
1960		646.4	1481.8	2453.8		
1961		662.2	1448.2	2460.6		
1962		694.8	1464.9	2535.4		
1963		705.1	1466.8	2521.7		
1964	10.3	755.5	1526.4	2764.9	1.5201	3.9615
1965	2.8	765.3	1548.7	2783.4	1.4755	3.9933
1966	2.9	781.3	1541.3	2824.9	1.4745	3.9646
1967	2.0	766.3	1501.7	2820.3	1.4140	3.4720
1968	2.1	791.6	1613.7	2931.8	1.4328	3.7794
1969	4.3	782.5	1494.2	2801.3	1.3076	3.1026
1970	5.4	740.3	1370.8	2670.4	1.2966	2.9216
1971	3.3	705.2	1247.6	2514.2	1.2314	2.6340
1972	3.0	771.9	1284.8	2543.9	1.2638	2.7141
1973	2.6	1186.7	1124.5	2257.2	1.3053	2.1741
1974		952.8	1097.9	2285.7		
1975				2083.7		

$\bar{q}_m(T)$	$Q_d(M/B)$	$Q_d(W/M)$	$Q_d(C/I)$	$Q_d(Slp)$	$Q_d(Ath)$	$Q_d(Wk)$
0.0439						
0.0531						
0.0666						
0.1778						
0.1311						
0.2240						
0.1790						
0.2686						
0.3754						
0.6146	112.4	307.1	63.1	78.8	6.9	32.2
0.7854	110.9	315.3	65.8	89.8	6.7	32.3
0.8410	112.6	318.8	65.9	93.4	7.0	38.3
1.1043	109.8	284.5	59.8	95.3	6.8	38.7
1.0792	113.1	315.5	59.5	105.1	8.1	36.2
1.6303	104.8	264.5	55.1	101.5	8.3	35.4
1.9117	105.6	252.6	54.8	96.0	8.4	37.5
2.1070	101.8	231.5	53.5	97.9	8.0	37.6
2.1251	106.0	242.3	49.3	96.3	15.5	33.7
2.2779	111.0	196.9	45.8	91.4	7.7	29.3
2.3363	84.7	127.3	30.6			
2.5244	93.3	183.3	32.7			

$q_d(C/T)$	$q_d(T)$	$q_d(Ath)$	$q_d(Wk)$	$q_d(Slp)$	$\bar{q}_d(M/B)$	$\bar{q}_d(W/M/C/I)$
					9.4616	13.6577
					9.4648	13.0685
					9.8360	13.0227
					9.8115	12.8488
1.5610	3.2297	0.0911	0.0436	0.0417	10.2147	12.9436
1.6376	3.2553	0.0499	0.0430	0.0469	10.1836	12.9979
1.6575	3.3035	0.0511	0.0502	0.0478	10.2307	12.8239
1.5284	3.0568	0.0450	0.0498	0.0488	9.7671	12.4059
1.5522	3.2446	0.0516	0.0459	0.0533	9.0971	13.2492
1.4753	3.8812	0.0631	0.0442	0.0510	8.5313	12.1922
1.4787	2.7769	0.0683	0.0461	0.0476	9.2047	11.0993
1.4668	2.6128	0.0556	0.0454	0.0479	13.9579	10.0305
1.3811	2.6449	0.0896	0.0402	0.0406	11.0571	10.2802
1.3162	2.3289	0.0493	0.0344	0.0439		8.9681
						8.7327

Year	$\bar{q}_d(T)$	$Q_c(M/B)$	$Q_c(W/M/C/I)$	$Q_c(Ath + Oth)$	$Q_c(Wk)$	$Q_c(Slp)$
1955	16.1143					
1956	15.9197					
1957	15.6068					
1958	15.0969 .					
1959	15.5235					
1960	13.6326					
1961	13.4415					
1962	13.6393					
1963	13.3663					
1964	14.6182	126.3	420.4	20.0	32.4	81.1
1965	14.5265	127.2	436.7	18.2	33.1	98.2
1966	14.6055	129.5	453.6	17.3	39.4	96.0
1967	14.4435	130.8	441.8	15.6	40.2	96.9
1968	14.8737	142.0	509.8	19.4	37.8	107.1
1969	14.0667	139.8	463.2	23.1	37.3	103.6
1970	13.2384	150.7	475.8	26.1	39.3	97.9
1971	12.3094	155.0	469.1	26.2	39.6	99.7
1972	12.3221	161.2	492.7	35.9	36.1	98.0
1973	10.8473	164.6	445.6	32.3	32.5	93.0
1974	10.8128					
1975	9.7773					

Year	$\bar{q}_c(T)$	$\bar{q}_c(M/B)$	$\bar{q}_c(W/M/C/I)$	$P_{M_1}(M/B)$	$P_{M_1}(W/M)$	$P_{M_1}(C/I)$
1955						
1956						
1957						
1958						
1959						
1960				157.1	176.8	113.0
1961				148.0	173.9	59.5
1962				136.1	161.6	26.2
1963				119.7	143.4	59.5
1964	15.2801	10.7261	13.8494	84.4	82.6	53.6
1965	15.3149	10.7298	13.8378	76.9	83.3	85.7
1966	15.6605	11.0273	13.8164	94.9	92.0	91.7
1967	15.5478	10.6630	13.4719	100.0	100.0	100.0
1968	16.3854	11.0771	14.6041	105.8	115.9	107.1
1969	15.6949	11.0665	13.6066	121.4	139.1	125.0
1970	14.9917	10.4398	12.7956	113.6	154.3	134.5
1971	14.5176	10.1917	12.2552	122.4	170.3	146.4
1972	15.4300	11.6917	13.2217	147.9	189.1	164.2
1973	14.9213	11.5918	12.1720	175.5	208.7	175.0
1974	14.3281	14.1776	12.1839	135.0	226.0	176.0
1975	12.2686	f	f	131.0	242.0	199.0

fNot available.

q_c(M/B)	q_c(W/M)	q_c(C/I)	q_c(T) (M/B + W/M + C/I)	$\bar{Q}_c$(T)[c]	$\bar{Q}_c$(M/B)[d]	(W/M/C/I)[e]
1.7074	4.5788	1.6175	3.5956	2890.1	793.3	1633.2
1.6911	4.6519	1.7265	3.7232	2934.4	806.4	1648.8
1.6961	4.7461	1.8087	3.8033	3029.1	842.2	1660.6
1.6846	4.5701	1.7183	3.7135	3035.9	828.2	1630.8
1.7987	5.2824	1.7929	4.1385	3229.8	874.1	1778.7
1.7445	4.6316	1.8307	3.8556	3125.6	886.7	1667.5
1.8503	4.6949	1.8859	3.9138	3024.1	849.6	1580.3
1.8752	4.5490	1.8989	3.8659	2965.2	842.5	1524.3
1.9218	4.7401	1.9468	3.9903	3185.6	980.5	1652.5
1.9360	4.2285	1.7964	3.6888	3104.9	985.59	1526.2
				3028.8	1221.7	1531.8

P_{M_1} (W/M/C/I)	P_{M_1}(T)	P_W(Gen)	P_W(Total footwear)	P_W(M/B)	P_W(W/M)	P_W(C/I)
	150.6	87.8	74.0			
	169.0	90.7	78.7			
	172.0	93.3	79.9			
	97.0	94.6	80.5			
	167.9	94.8	85.4			
97.0	115.5	94.9	87.6	84.8	89.7	86.5
180.3	153.6	94.5	88.0	84.8	90.2	86.8
157.6	135.1	94.8	88.9	86.5	90.8	87.5
113.6	110.2	94.5	88.7	86.5	90.3	87.5
82.6	83.3	94.7	88.9	86.8	90.3	87.8
84.1	77.4	96.6	90.7	89.4	91.6	90.1
92.4	93.5	99.8	96.8	97.0	96.8	96.6
100.0	100.0	100.0	100.0	100.0	100.0	100.0
117.7	154.4	102.5	104.8	103.6	105.3	107.4
140.0	131.5	106.5	109.5	108.1	110.1	112.9
154.5	140.5	110.4	113.0	111.4	113.7	117.0
170.5	154.8	113.9	116.8	115.7	117.2	119.8
187.9	173.8	119.1	124.5	125.9	123.3	126.1
208.3	197.0	134.7	130.5	137.9	125.4	130.2
		160.1	140.0	150.4	132.8	138.5
		174.9	147.8	159.3	140.2	143.7

[c] Domestic + import value/CPI footwear.
[d] Domestic + import value/CPI (men's street shoes).
[e] Domestic + import value/CPI (women's street shoes).

Year	$P_W(Slp)$	$P_W(Ath)$	$P_W(Wk)$	$P_W(Oth)^g$	$p_{m_1}(M/B)$	$p_{m_1}(W/M)$
1955						
1956						
1957						
1958						
1959						
1960					165.5	186.3
1961					157.3	184.0
1962					143.6	170.5
1963					126.7	151.7
1964	80.3	72.7	88.5	72.7	89.1	87.2
1965	83.4	127.3	90.1	127.3	79.6	86.2
1966	93.6	129.8	96.4	129.8	95.1	92.2
1967	100.0	100.0	100.0	100.0	100.0	100.0
1968	101.9	117.3	102.2	117.3	103.2	113.1
1969	112.1	92.0	106.6	92.0	114.0	130.6
1970	117.5	158.0	110.8	158.0	102.9	140.0
1971	116.4	229.2	118.3	229.2	107.5	149.5
1972	133.8	125.2	129.9	125.5	124.2	158.8
1973	145.9	175.2	145.4	175.2	130.3	155.0
1974					84.3	141.2
1975					74.9	138.4

Year	$P_{M_2}(Ath)$	$P_{M_2}(Wk)$	$P_{M_2}(Oth)$	$p_{m_2}(M/B)$	$p_{m_2}(W/M)$	$p_{m_2}(C/I)$
1955						
1956						
1957						
1958						
1959						
1960						
1961						
1962						
1963						
1964	105.7	97.7	40.0	102.9	87.6	117.2
1965	99.1	92.1	24.4	99.6	94.6	103.3
1966	102.7	93.5	102.3	97.7	91.8	94.4
1967	100.0	100.0	100.0	100.0	100.0	100.0
1968	95.6	96.9	98.7	98.1	119.1	121.8
1969	86.3	99.3	105.8	100.6	124.6	125.2
1970	83.7	108.0	122.3	100.1	125.6	123.9
1971	77.8	109.2	128.8	103.2	124.0	124.9
1972	84.0	118.4	122.1	116.1	120.6	127.0
1973	85.5	132.5	163.8	116.3	111.7	115.9
1974						
1975						

^{g}Not WPI, but computed as simple unit-value index.

$p_{m_1}(C/I)$	$p_{m_1}(W/M/C/I)$	$p_{m_1}(T)$	$P_{M_2}(M/B)$	$P_{M_2}(W/M)$	$P_{M_2}(C/I)$	$P_{M_2}(Slp)$
		171.5				
		186.3				
		184.4				
		102.5				
		177.1				
91.1	102.2	121.7				
91.9	190.8	162.5				
92.3	166.2	142.5				
92.6	120.2	116.6				
92.7	87.2	88.0	97.4	83.0	111.0	94.0
93.3	87.1	80.1	96.2	91.4	99.8	86.1
96.8	92.6	93.7	97.5	91.6	94.2	84.2
100.0	100.0	100.0	100.0	100.0	100.0	100.0
104.8	113.9	150.6	100.6	122.1	124.8	96.7
106.0	131.5	123.5	107.1	132.7	133.3	104.2
106.0	139.9	127.3	110.5	138.7	136.8	127.6
105.2	149.7	135.9	117.6	141.2	142.3	131.1
105.9	157.8	145.9	138.3	143.6	151.3	141.6
96.7	154.6	146.3	156.6	150.5	156.1	156.3
109.9	139.1	199.0				
113.8	137.2	211.0				

$p_{m_2}(Slp)$	$p_{m_2}(Ath)$	$p_{m_2}(Wk)$	$p_{m_2}(Oth)$	$p_d(M/B)$	$p_d(W/M)$	$p_d(C/I)$
				89.4	94.5	91.1
				89.7	95.4	91.9
				91.2	95.8	92.3
				91.5	95.6	92.6
99.3	111.6	103.2	42.2	91.7	95.4	92.7
89.1	102.6	95.3	25.3	92.5	94.8	93.3
84.4	102.9	93.7	102.5	97.2	97.0	96.8
100.0	100.0	100.0	100.0	100.0	100.0	100.0
94.3	93.3	94.5	96.3	101.1	102.7	104.8
97.8	81.0	93.2	99.3	101.5	103.4	106.0
115.6	75.8	97.8	110.8	100.9	103.0	106.0
115.1	68.3	95.9	113.1	101.6	102.9	105.2
118.9	70.5	99.4	102.5	105.7	103.5	105.9
116.0	63.5	98.4	121.6	102.4	93.1	96.7
				93.9	82.9	
				91.1	80.2	

Year	p_d(W/M/C/I)	p_d(T)	p_d(Slp)	p_d(Ath)	p_d(Wk)	p_d(Oth)
1955		84.6				
1956		86.8				
1957		85.6				
1958		85.1				
1959		90.1				
1960	94.1	92.3				
1961	95.1	93.1				
1962	95.4	93.8				
1963	95.2	93.9				
1964	96.0	93.9	84.8	76.8	93.5	76.8
1965	94.6	93.9	86.3	131.8	93.3	131.8
1966	97.0	97.0	93.8	130.0	96.6	130.0
1967	100.0	100.0	100.0	100.0	100.0	100.0
1968	102.9	102.2	99.4	114.7	99.7	114.7
1969	103.7	102.8	105.3	86.4	100.1	86.4
1970	103.4	102.4	106.4	143.1	100.4	143.1
1971	103.2	102.5	102.2	202.2	103.9	201.2
1972	103.8	104.5	112.3	105.4	109.1	105.4
1973	93.5	96.9	108.3	130.0	107.9	130.0
1974	82.5	87.4				
1975	80.2	84.5				

Year	p_{m_2}/p_d(W/M)	p_{m_2}/p_d(C/I)	p_{m_2}/p_d(Slp)	p_{m_2}/p_d(Ath)	p_{m_2}/p_d(Wk)	p_{m_2}/p_d(Oth)
1955						
1956						
1957						
1958						
1959						
1960						
1961						
1962						
1963						
1964	91.8	126.4	117.1	145.3	110.4	54.9
1965	99.8	110.7	103.2	77.8	102.1	19.2
1966	94.6	97.5	90.0	79.2	97.0	78.8
1967	100.0	100.0	100.0	100.0	100.0	100.0
1968	116.0	116.2	94.9	81.3	94.8	84.0
1969	120.5	118.1	92.9	93.8	93.1	114.9
1970	121.9	116.9	108.6	53.0	97.4	77.4
1971	120.5	118.7	112.6	34.0	92.3	56.2
1972	116.5	120.0	105.9	66.9	91.1	97.2
1973	120.0	119.8	107.1	48.8	91.2	93.5
1974						
1975						

p_{m_1}/p_d(M/B)	p_{m_1}/p_d(W/M)	p_{m_1}/p_d(C/I)	p_{m_1}/p_d(W/M/C/I)	p_{m_1}/p_d(T)	p_{m_2}/p_d(M/B)
				203.4	
				214.6	
				215.4	
				120.4	
				196.6	
185.1	197.1	91.1	108.6	131.9	
175.4	192.8	91.9	200.6	174.5	
157.5	178.0	92.3	174.2	151.9	
138.5	158.7	92.6	126.3	124.6	
97.2	91.4	92.7	90.8	93.7	112.2
86.1	90.9	93.3	92.1	85.3	107.7
97.8	95.1	96.8	95.5	96.6	100.5
100.0	100.0	100.0	100.0	100.0	100.0
102.1	110.1	104.8	110.7	147.4	97.0
112.3	126.3	106.0	126.8	120.1	99.1
102.0	135.9	106.0	135.3	124.3	99.2
105.8	145.3	105.2	145.1	132.6	101.6
117.5	153.4	105.9	152.0	139.6	109.8
127.2	166.5	96.7	165.4	150.9	113.6
89.8	170.3		168.6	227.7	
82.2	172.6		171.1	249.7	

p_{m_2}/p_d(T)	p_c(T)	p_c(M/B)	p_c(W/M/C/I)	p_c(Ath)	p_c(Wk)
93.9	93.9	92.5	94.6	82.6	93.6
101.7	94.0	93.1	94.7	116.8	93.3
97.4	96.8	97.2	96.0	113.5	96.5
100.0	100.0	100.0	100.0	100.0	100.0
107.9	102.8	100.9	102.3	108.0	93.7
110.4	103.6	101.4	105.4	86.1	99.9
111.2	103.3	100.8	105.1	123.6	100.3
110.7	103.3	101.7	104.8	162.7	103.7
110.4	105.3	106.5	105.2	96.8	108.9
113.4	97.8	103.4	95.0	113.4	108.0

Year	p_e(Slp)	y	T	p_ℓ	w
1955		1795	1	89.1	1.50
1956		1839	2	93.1	1.57
1957		1844	3	89.3	1.58
1958		1831	4	90.2	1.60
1959		1881	5	109.1	1.64
1960		1883	6	98.8	1.68
1961		1909	7	101.7	1.72
1962		1969	8	103.8	1.77
1963		2015	9	97.8	1.81
1964	84.9	2126	10	98.5	1.87
1965	86.4	2239	11	101.4	1.88
1966	93.7	2335	12	110.0	1.87
1967	100.0	2403	13	100.0	2.01
1968	99.4	2486	14	99.6	2.13
1969	105.2	2534	15	102.1	2.17
1970	106.5	2610	16	97.6	2.20
1971	102.3	2683	17	98.8	2.22
1972	112.4	2799	18	117.8	2.21
1973	108.4	2945	19	118.9	2.02
1974		2845	20	96.4	1.82
1975		3150	21	86.6	1.78

Year	p_a(W/M)	p_a(C/I)	p_a(T)	pce	c_u(M)
1955					
1956					
1957					
1958					
1959					
1960					88.0
1961					88.7
1962					90.2
1963					90.8
1964	103.4	100.0	101.7	1976	91.0
1965	102.0	99.0	101.5	2076	88.8
1966	99.3	96.9	98.5	2162	85.6
1967	100.0	100.0	100.0	2203	84.4
1968	100.3	104.0	101.1	2297	86.1
1969	99.8	103.8	100.8	2356	84.6
1970	98.4	104.6	100.4	2367	87.8
1971	96.6	103.7	99.1	2430	87.6
1972	93.9	100.2	96.4	2554	89.3
1973	85.7	90.3	88.3	2653	88.2
1974					79.4
1975					70.8

p_{hs}	k	k(Slp)	k_n	k_n(Slp)	p_a(M/B)
98.1	117.3	127.5	85.3	91.7	99.9
122.2	121.3	138.7	90.7	108.4	99.1
149.8	146.5	122.3	103.7	105.0	97.8
100.0	140.0	118.3	102.8	104.0	100.0
103.5	229.7	114.7	158.7	95.6	101.1
116.5	161.4	189.7	107.5	85.4	101.6
94.5	166.9	129.4	110.1	138.7	101.8
101.1	174.9	103.9	133.6	94.4	101.4
179.4	198.7	201.0	140.0	177.4	98.8
188.5	205.0(p)[h]	230.0(p)	145.0(p)	201.2(p)	91.5

c_u(W)	c_u(C)	c_u(T)	c_u(Slp)	c_u(Oth)	c_u(Ath)
		75.7			
		75.9			
		75.8			
		77.4			
		77.1			
80.3		76.9	66.5	81.2	79.1
78.2		75.4	63.4	73.4	72.2
84.2		78.8	72.5	67.4	77.0
88.2		75.7	66.6	54.0	74.3
79.3	75.5	77.7	67.7	62.4	52.9
84.4	84.9	81.9	77.4	i	54.1
85.8	83.5	80.2	78.3	i	57.7
78.1	76.4	78.4	79.7	49.8	79.2
85.8	78.1	82.7	80.7	51.4	88.8
75.5	76.6	77.8	76.4	83.3	86.8
72.9	72.3	76.1	73.6	65.8	87.8
71.3	71.0	77.0	79.1	40.6	82.7
73.4	80.3	78.2	75.7	25.2	84.5
71.0	71.9	77.2	82.7	30.4	90.0
72.7		71.9			
78.6		68.4			

[h] p means preliminary.
[i] Not computed.

Year	Total resident United States population (thousands)	United States resident male civilian population, 10 years and over (thousands)	United States resident female civilian population, 10 years and over (thousands)	United States resident children population, 0–9 years (thousands)
1955	165.069			
1956	168.088			
1957	171.187			
1958	174.149			
1959	177.135			
1960	179.979	68.321	73.437	35.057
1961	182.992	69.965	75.274	35.545
1962	185.771	70.639	76.466	36.026
1963	188.483	71.870	77.833	36.325
1964	191.141	73.962	77.527	40.400
1965	193.526	75.153	78.948	40.202
1966	195.576	76.372	80.408	39.781
1967	197.457	77.663	81.953	39.096
1968	199.399	78.911	83.468	38.327
1969	201.385	80.123	85.236	37.318
1970	203.810	81.379	86.445	37.055
1971	206.230	82.663	87.891	36.492
1972	208.164	83.861	89.257	35.725
1973	209.844	85.017	90.568	34.819
1974	211.389	86.171	91.848	33.875
1975	213.137	87.284	93.117	33.231

Females + children (thousands)	CPI (total nonrubber footwear)	CPI (men's street shoes)	CPI (women's street shoes)	$V_M(T)$
	71.6			10,920
	75.4			15,075
	77.8			19,597
	79.0			30,040
	82.2			38,995
108.494	85.1	85.2	84.9	46,564
110.819	85.9	86.3	86.0	50,330
112.492	87.1	87.0	87.2	67,453
114.158	88.0	86.6	87.9	78,036
117.927	88.4	87.0	88.3	96,834
119.150	90.0	89.4	89.6	116,475
120.189	95.3	95.6	94.9	152,087
121.049	100.0	100.0	100.0	215,622
121.795	105.3	104.1	107.4	328,442
122.554	111.8	109.5	114.8	426,938
123.500	117.7	114.8	120.7	541,789
124.383	121.5	119.6	123.4	666,181
124.982	124.9	123.6	126.3	811,603
125.387	130.2	132.6	129.4	935,356
125.723	138.1	141.9	135.2	982,900
126.348	161.2	147.6	139.0	1,135,300

Year	V_M(M/B)	V_M(W/M)	V_M(C/I)	v_m(T)	v_m(M/B)	v_m(W/M)
1955				0.0066		
1956				0.0897		
1957				0.1145		
1958				0.1725		
1959				0.2201		
1960	24,195			0.2587	0.3541	
1961	24,126			0.2750	0.3448	
1962	29,058			0.3631	0.4114	
1963	30,418			0.4140	0.4232	
1964	34,411	53,277	1359	0.5066	0.4652	0.6872
1965	36,698	59,177	2604	0.6019	0.4883	0.7496
1966	47,218	79,380	4542	0.7776	0.6183	0.9872
1967	61,803	122,862	6174	1.0920	0.7958	1.4992
1968	89,824	199,468	8430	1.6472	1.1383	2.3898
1969	124,958	250,785	13,952	2.1200	1.5596	2.9422
1970	150,611	326,291	17,045	2.6583	1.8507	3.7746
1971	191,663	395,708	19,381	3.2303	2.3186	4.5023
1972	240,021	471,143	27,867	3.8989	2.8621	5.2785
1973	276,757	533,589	24,474	4.4574	3.2553	5.8916
1974	300,600	585,200	27,800			
1975	327,201	657,600	29,650	4.9364	3.5139	6.5119

Year	$V_M + V_d$(M/B)	$V_M + V_d$ (W/M/C/I)	P_L	W	V_m(W/M/C/I)	Y_r
1955			78.2	1.32		343,327
1956			84.4	1.42		360,171
1957			83.3	1.47		365,983
1958			85.3	1.51		368,159
1959			103.4	1.55		386,386
1960			93.8	1.59		394,638
1961			96.1	1.63		406,723
1962			98.4	1.68		425,240
1963			92.4	1.71		441,226
1964	690	1442	93.3	1.77	54,636	471,578
1965	721	1477	98.0	1.82	61,781	500,783
1966	805	1576	109.8	1.87	83,922	526,597
1967	828	1631	100.0	2.01	129,036	546,341
1968	910	1910	102.1	2.18	207,898	567,176
1969	971	1914	108.7	2.31	264,737	577,765
1970	975	1907	107.7	2.43	343,336	594,754
1971	1008	1881	112.5	2.53	415,089	615,361
1972	1212	2087	140.3	2.63	499,010	640,464
1973	1307	1975	160.1	2.72	558,063	678,974
1974						665,913
1975						667,928

v_m(C/I)	Y	Y^*	V_d(T)	V_d(M/B)	V_d(W/M/C/I)	$V_M + V_d$(T)
	275,348	1666	1968			1979
	293,179	1743	2106			2121
	308,524	1801	2135			2155
	318,826	1831	2116			2146
	337,315	1905	2348			2387
	350,044	1937	2150	548	133	2197
	364,424	1984	2165	601	131	2215
	385,267	2065	2254	562	133	2321
	404,604	2138	2237	610	132	2315
0.0336	438,096	2283	2458	656	1387	2555
0.0645	473,240	2436	2525	684	1416	2641
0.1142	511,852	2604	2735	758	1492	2887
0.1579	546,341	2749	2820	766	1502	3036
0.2199	590,997	2945	3073	820	1702	3401
0.3739	634,386	3130	3067	846	1650	3494
0.4599	691,997	3376	3018	825	1564	3560
0.5311	746,433	3605	2937	816	1466	3603
0.7800	802,501	3843	3167	972	1588	3979
0.7029	903,714	4295	3107	1030	1417	4043
	983,553	4642	3200	1433	1458	
0.8922	1,076,700	5040	3080			

P_d (W/M/C/I)	Q_M (W/M/C/I)	CPI (general)	Q_M(T)	Q_d(T)	p_{m_4}(T)	p_{m_4}(W/M)
		80.2				
		81.4				
		84.3				
		86.6				
		87.3				
89.3	7.8	88.7				
90.3	9.8	89.6			65.6	64.8
90.4	14.4	90.6			70.1	69.4
90.0	19.0	91.7	41.8	599.1	74.1	72.9
90.9	50.2	92.9	67.7	610.9	80.9	79.7
91.4	53.6	94.5	82.3	623.7	83.5	82.6
96.8	68.9	97.2	91.6	638.9	93.7	93.5
100.0	97.5	100.0	124.6	596.9	100.0	100.0
105.5	134.8	104.2	170.2	639.5	102.0	101.9
110.4	143.6	109.8	193.8	573.8	100.2	100.1
114.2	168.4	116.3	229.5	560.1	99.4	99.1
117.5	184.1	121.3	256.3	533.7	98.4	98.4
123.6	201.1	125.3	278.1	546.0	100.8	101.0
125.9	202.9	133.1	283.0	484.6	103.9	104.8
		147.7	334.5	301.7		
		161.2	290.4	372.5		

Year	$p_{m_4}(M/B)$	$p_{m_4}(C/I)$	$p_{m_4}/p_d(T)$	$p_{m_4}/p_d(M/B)$	$p_{m_4}/p_d(W/M)$
1955					
1956					
1957					
1958					
1959					
1960					
1961	66.9	70.1	70.5	74.6	67.9
1962	70.9	75.3	74.7	77.7	72.4
1963	75.6	78.6	78.9	82.6	76.3
1964	82.3	88.8	86.2	89.7	83.5
1965	84.7	90.4	88.9	91.6	87.1
1966	94.1	95.4	96.6	96.8	96.4
1967	100.0	100.0	100.0	100.0	100.0
1968	101.9	102.5	99.8	100.8	99.2
1969	100.3	100.6	97.5	98.8	96.8
1970	99.5	100.7	97.1	98.6	96.2
1971	98.1	101.9	96.0	96.6	95.6
1972	99.8	105.5	96.5	94.4	97.6
1973	101.3	110.0	107.2	98.9	112.6
1974					
1975					

DATA SOURCES

Import quantity and value are from U.S. Foreign Trade, *Imports by TSUSA Commodity and Country,* "Consumption and General Quantity and Value," U.S. Department of Commerce, Social and Economic Statistics Administration, Bureau of the Census, various years.[82]

Disposable per capita income and personal consumption expenditure are taken from U.S. Department of Commerce, Bureau of Economic Analysis, *National Income and Product Accounts of the United States.*[81]

Resident civilian population at mid-year comes from Department of Commerce, Bureau of the Census, *Current Population Reports,* Series P25.[79]

Capacity utilization rate is computed by the American Footwear Industry Association (AFIA) in the following manner: Total effective capacity is the sum of the monthly production peaks for each type of footwear over a 36 month period ending December 31 of the year involved. See *Footwear Manual, 1974.*[75]

Capital expenditure and expenditure on new machinery and equipment, production workers in nonrubber footwear, and slippers are from *Annual Survey of Manufactures, Census of Manufactures,* U.S. Department of Commerce.[80]

Domestic WPI for footwear and components thereof and for other commodities come from U.S. Department of Labor, BLS, *Employment and Earnings,* various issues.[83] Each of the price series is divided by the all-consumption WPI to obtain relative price.

Domestic footwear production is taken from U.S. Bureau of the Census, *Current Industrial Reports,* Series M31A 13, "Shoes and Slippers" (annual except for census years).[77] Value of domestic footwear production is from U.S. Bureau of the Census, *Annual Survey of Manufactures* and, for census years, from *Census of Manufactures.*

Value and pairs of footwear exports are from U.S. Bureau of the Census, *Exports of Domestic and Foreign Merchandise Commodity By Country of Destination.*[78]

REFERENCES

I. BOOKS

1. Bain, J. S., *Barriers to New Competition*. Cambridge, Massachusetts: Harvard Univ. Press, 1956.
2. Bain, J. S., *Essays on Price Theory and Industrial Concentration*. Boston, Massachusetts: Little Brown, 1972.
3. Bryce, M., *Industrial Development*. New York: McGraw-Hill, 1960.
4. Corden, W. M., *Trade Policy and Economic Welfare*. London and New York: Oxford Univ. Press: (Clarendon) 1974.
5. Houthakker, H. S., and Taylor, L. D., *Consumer Demand in the United States, 1929–1970*. Cambridge, Massachusetts: Harvard Univ. Press, 1966.
6. Leamer, E. D., and Stern, R. M., *Quantitative International Economics*. Boston, Massachusetts: Allyn and Bacon, 1970.
7. Lombardi, J. W., *The Italian Footwear Industry: An Empirical Analysis*. Bern: Lang and Co., 1971.
8. MacPhee, C. R., *Restrictions on International Trade in Steel*. Lexington, Massachusetts: Lexington Books, 1974.
9. Pratten, C., and Dean, R. M., *The Economies of Large-Scale Production in British Industry*. London and New York: Cambridge Univ. Press, 1965.
10. Silverman, H. A., *Studies in Industrial Organization*. London, 1945.
11. Wiles, P., *Price, Cost and Output*. Oxford: Blackwell, 1956.

II. REPORTS AND UNPUBLISHED MATERIALS

12. Bale, M. D., *Adjustment to Freer Trade: An Analysis of the Adjustment Assistance Provisions of the Trade Expansion Act of 1962*, prepared for the Manpower Administration, U.S. Dept. of Labor, Washington, D.C.

13. Bergsten, C. F., *Trade Adjustment Assistance, Hearings of the House Subcommittee on Foreign Economic Policy, U.S. Congress*. Washington, D.C.: U.S. Gov't. Printing Office (1972).

14. Bergsten, C. F., *The Cost of Import Restrictions to American Consumers*. A pamphlet published by the American Importers Association, New York (no publication date indicated).

15. Brimmer, A. F., "Import Controls and Domestic Inflation" paper presented at the Economics Seminar, Univ. of Maryland (November 11, 1970).

16. Bureau of International Labor Affairs, *Survey of Workers Displaced by Import Competition* (internal study), U.S. Department of Labor, Washington, D.C. (1972).

17. Bureau of International Labor Affairs (BILA), *Trade Adjustment Assistance for Workers—Experience to Date*, U.S. Department of Labor, Washington, D.C. (December 31, 1974).

18. Cohn, S., *International Comparisons of Productivity and Labor Costs in the Nonrubber Footwear Industry*, prepared for the U.S. Dept. of Labor, Bureau of Labor Statistics, Washington, D.C. (1974).

19. Commission on International Trade and Investment (Williams Commission) and the Trade Adjustment Assistance Hearings of the Subcommittee on Foreign Economic Policy of the House Committee on Foreign Affairs (April and May 1972).

20. Committee on Industrial Organization, *Report of the Leather Footwear Industry*, Dublin (1962).

21. Duchesneau, T., and Mandell, L., *The Diffusion of Innovation: A Longitudinal Study*. Study in progress for the Nat. Sci. Foundation, Washington, D.C.

22. Floyd, J. E., *The Effects of United States Trade Restrictions on Economic Efficiency*, prepared for the Bur. of Internat. Labor Affairs, U.S. Dept. of Labor, Washington, D.C.

23. Fooks, M. M., "Trade Adjustment Assistance" in *United States International Policy in an Interdependent World*, report to the President submitted by the Commission on Int. Trade and Investment Policy, Copendium I (July 1972).

24. Fulda, C. H., "Adjustment to Hardship Caused by Imports: the New Decisions of the Tariff Commission and the Need for Legislative Clarification," *Michigan Law Review*, **70**, No. 5, 815 (1972).

25. General Plywood Corp., TEA-F-6 (1964).

26. Jacks, S. M., *Productivity Issues in the Domestic Shoe Industry*, prepared for the Nat. Commission on Productivity, Washington, D.C. (August 27, 1971).

27. Jaffe, E. D., and Nagel, H. L., "Import Competition and Adjustment Assistance," paper delivered at the *Eastern Economic Association Meetings*, Albany, New York (October 1974).

28. Jondrow, J. *et al.*, *Removing Restrictions on Imports of Steel*, prepared for the Public Res. Inst., a Division of the Center for Naval Analyses, Arlington, Virginia (1975).

29. Kemp, B. A., "More on Measures of Market Structure" in *Systems Evaluation*

Group Research Contribution No. 6, Center for Naval Analyses, Washington, D.C., The Franklin Institute.

30. Magee, S. P., "How Much of Current Unemployment Did We Import" and "The Welfare Effects of Restrictions on U.S. Trade" in *Brookings Papers on Economic Activity* Nos. 2 and 3 (1972).

31. McCarthy, J. E., *Trade Adjustment Assistance: Case Study of the Massachusetts Shoe Industry,* unpublished Ph.D. dissertation, Fletcher School of Law and Diplomacy, Tufts Univ. (1974).

32. Merrill Lynch, Pierce, Fenner, and Smith, *The Footwear Industry,* A Special Report, New York, New York (1973).

33. National Association of Manufacturers, *Trade Adjustment Assistance,* Staff Rep., Washington, D.C. (1972).

34. National Association of Manufacturers (NAM), *Trade Adjustment Assistance,* Staff Report, Washington, D.C. (1972).

35. National Planning Association, *U.S. Foreign Economic Policy for the 1970's: A New Approach to New Realities,* Washington, D.C. (1972).

36. National Tile and Manufacturing Co., TEA-F-5 (1964).

37. Priebe, T., *An Analysis of Diffusion in Manufacturing Innovations in the New England Shoe Industry,* unpublished M.A. thesis, MIT (1965).

38. *Report of the Task Force on Nonrubber Footwear,* Washington, D.C. (1971).

39. Stocking, G., and Heflebower, R., "Readings in Industrial Organization and Public Policy."

III. ARTICLES AND PERIODICALS

40. Adelman, M. A., "Differential Rates and Changes in Concentration," *Review of Economics and Statistics* (February 1959).

41. Adelman, M. A., "The Measurement of Industrial Concentration," *Review of Economics and Statistics* (November 1951).

42. Bain, J. S., "Relation of Profit Rate to Industry Concentration," *Quarterly Journal of Economics* (August 1951).

43. Bain, J. S., "Survival Ability as a Test of Efficiency," *American Economic Review* (May 1969).

44. Bale, M. D., Comment, *Southern Economic Journal* (1973).

45. Bale, M. D., "Adjustment Assistance under the Trade Expansion Act of 1962," *Journal of International Law and Economics* 9 (April 1974).

46. Banner, T. K., "In Major Part—The New Causation Problem in the Trade Agreements Program," *Texas Law Review* 44 (1966).

47. Basevi, G., "The Restrictive Effect of the U.S. Tariff and Its Welfare Value," in *American Economic Review* (September 1968).

48. Blair, J. M., "Statistical Measures of Concentration in Business: Problems of Compiling and Interpretation," *Bulletin of the Oxford Institute of Statistics* (November 1956).

49. Bratt, H. A., "Assisting the Economic Recovery of Import-Injured Firms," *Law and Policy in International Business* 6 (1974).

50. *Business Week* (June 10, 1972).
51. Currie, J. M., Murphy, J. A., and Schmitz, A., "The Concept of Economic Surplus and Its Uses in Economic Analysis," *Economic Journal* (December 1971).
52. Fieleke, N. S., "The Cost of Tariffs to Consumers," *New England Economic Review* (September–October 1971).
53. Floyd, J. E., "The Overvaluation of the Dollar: A Note on the International Price Mechanism," *American Economic Review* (March 1965).
54. Hart, P. E., and Prais, J. S., "The Analysis of Business Concentration: A Statistical Approach," *Journal of the Royal Statistical Society* Ser. A, Part II (1956).
55. Horowitz, A., and Horowitz, I., "Firms in a Declining Industry: The Brewing Case," *Journal of Industrial Economics* (March 1965).
56. Houthakker, H. S., and Magee, S. P., "Income and Price Elasticities in World Trade," *Review of Economics and Statistics* (May 1969).
57. Johnson, H., "The Economic Approach to Social Questions," *Public Interest* (Summer, 1968).
58. Mishan, M. J., "What is Producer Surplus?" *American Economic Review* (December 1968).
59. *New York Times*, "Senate Approves Trade Bill Giving Benefit to Soviet" (December 14, 1974).
60. *New York Times*, "Shoe Industry Finding Imports Painful to Bear, Easier to Wear" (July 3, 1969).
61. *New York Times*, "Senate Approves Trade Bill Giving Benefit to Soviet," December 14, 1974.
62. *New York Times*, "Trade Bill Fate in Senate is Linked to Amendment," December 11, 1974; *Long Island Press*, "The Trade Bill: A Study in Irresponsibility," December 31, 1974; *Long Island Press*, "Labor Sees Loss of Jobs in Trade Bill," January 26, 1975; and others, too numerous to list.
63. Prais, J. S., "The Statistical Conditions for a Change in Business Concentration," *Review of Economics and Statistics* (August 1958).
64. Price, J. E., and Thornblade, J. B., "U.S. Import Demand Functions Disaggregated by Country and Commodity," *Southern Economic Journal* (July 1972).
65. Rosenbluth, G., "Measures of Concentration," *Business Concentration and Price Policy*. Princeton, New Jersey: Princeton Univ. Press for the Nat. Bur. of Economic Res. (1955).
66. Ross, N., "Management and the Size of the Firm," *Review of Economic Studies* No. 3 (1952).
67. Saving, T. R., "Estimation of Optimum Size of Plant by the Survivor Technique," *Quarterly Journal of Economics* (November 1961).
68. Shepherd, W. G., "Economic Rent and the Industry Supply Curve," *Southern Economic Journal* (December 1971).
69. Shepherd, W. G., "What Does the Survivor Technique Show About Economies of Scale," *Southern Economic Journal* (July 1967).
70. Simon, H. A., and Bonini, C., "The Size Distribution of Business Firms," *American Economic Review* (September 1958).
71. Stigler, G. J., "The Economies of Scale," *Journal of Law and Economics* (October 1958).
72. *Wall Street Journal*, "Expansion Minded Retailers Take Over Stores Left Vacant by Recession Victims" (August 5, 1975).

73. Weiss, L., "The Survival Technique and the Extent of Suboptimal Capacity," *Journal of Political Economy* (June 1964).
74. Williamson, O. E., "Allocative Efficiency and the Limits of Antitrust," *American Economic Review* (May 1969).

IV. PUBLIC DOCUMENTS

75. American Footwear Industry Association, *Footwear Manual* (1974).
76. U.S. Bureau of the Census, *Annual Survey of Manufactures* (various years).
77. U.S. Bureau of the Census, *Current Industrial Reports,* Series M31A, 13 "Shoes and Slippers" (various years).
78. U.S. Bureau of the Census, *Exports of Domestic and Foreign Merchandise Commodity by Country of Destination* (various years).
79. U.S. Dept. of Commerce, Bureau of the Census, *Current Population Reports* Ser. P25.
80. U.S. Dept. of Commerce, *Census of Manufactures, Annual Survey of Manufactures* (various years).
81. U.S. Dept. of Commerce, *National Income and Product Accounts of the United States*, Bureau of Economic Analysis (various years).
82. U.S. Dept. of Commerce, Social and Economic Statistics Administration, Bureau of the Census, U.S. Foreign Trade, *Imports by TSUSA Commodity and Country,* "Consumption and General Quantity and Value," various years.
83. U.S. Dept. of Labor, Bureau of Labor Statistics, *Employment and Earnings* (various years).
84. U.S. Dept. of Labor, Bureau of Labor Statistics, *Indexes of Output per Man-Hour—Selected Industries* (1972).
85. Buttweld Pipe, TEA-W-8 (1968).
86. Pianos, TEA-W-24 (1970).
87. Footwear for Women, TEA-W-237, Tariff Commission Publ. No. 686, p. 11 (1974).
88. Nonrubber Footwear, TEA-I-18 Tariff Commission Publ. No. 359 (1971).
89. Women's Shoes, TEA-F-10, Tariff Commission Pub. No. 323 (1970); TEA-W-15/18, Tariff Commission Publ. 323 (1970).
90. P. L. 93–618, Sect. 238.
91. P. L. 93–618.
92. H.R. Report No. 1818, 87th Congress, 2nd Session (1962); Senate Report No. 2059, 87th Congress, 2nd Session (1962).
93. H.R. 18970, 91st Congress, 2nd session, 1970, the so-called "Trade Bill"; H.R. 16920, 91st Congress, 2nd session (1970), the "Mills Bill."
94. H.R. 6767, 93rd Congress, 1st session (1973).
95. Trade Act of 1974, P. L. 93–618 (January 3, 1975), in particular chapters 2, 3, 4 of Title II.
96. Transmission Towers, Tariff Commission Publ. No. 298 (November 1969).
97. U.S. Tariff Commission, "Report to the President on Investigation No. TEA-I-18 Under Section 301(b) of the Trade Expansion Act of 1962," Washington, D.C. (January 1971).
98. Public Research Institute, *Removing Restrictions on Import of Steel,* Arlington, Virginia (1975).

INDEX

A page reference followed by an n indicates a footnote. An italic page reference indicates a table or figure.

A
B 7
C 8
D 9
E 0
F 1
G 2
H 3
I 4
J 5